Thomas Sowell

THE LENGTHENING
SHADOW OF SLAVERY

THE LENGTHENING SHADOW OF SLAVERY

A Historical Justification for Affirmative Action
for Blacks in Higher Education

JOHN E. FLEMING
with the assistance of
JULIUS HOBSON, JR.
JOHN McCLENDON
HERSCHELLE REED

INSTITUTE FOR THE STUDY OF EDUCATIONAL POLICY
HOWARD UNIVERSITY

Published for ISEP by
HOWARD UNIVERSITY PRESS
Washington, D.C.
1976

Library of Congress Cataloging in Publication Data
Fleming, John, 1944-   The lengthening shadow of slavery.

    Bibliography: p.
    Includes index.
    1. Afro-Americans—Education (Higher)—History. 2. Slavery in the United States. 3. United States—Race question. 4. Afro-Americans—Civil rights. I. Howard University, Washington, D.C. Institute for the Study of Educational Policy. II. Title.
LC2781.F57   370'.973   76-21656   ISBN 0-88258-074-4.

Acknowledgments are gratefully extended to the following:

    Arno Press—for excerpts from *Evolution of the Negro College,* by Dwight O. W. Holmes, reprinted by Arno Press, Inc., 1969.

    Citadel Press, Inc.—for excerpts from *Documentary History of the Negro People in the United States,* Volume II, by Herbert Aptheker.

    Joan Daves—for an excerpt from the "I Have a Dream" speech of Martin Luther King, Jr., copyright © 1963 by Martin Luther King, Jr.

    University of North Carolina Press—for excerpts from *The Negro in the American Revolution,* by Benjamin Quarles and the Institute of Early American History and Culture, for whom it was published.

    This report was made possible by a grant from the Ford Foundation

ACKNOWLEDGMENTS

This monograph was made possible by the support of the Institute for the Study of Educational Policy of Howard University. Appreciation is extended to the Director, Kenneth S. Tollett, who provided more than ample support as the study progressed. I also wish to thank members of the Institute's Advisory Board for their review of the manuscript and positive criticism. Appreciation is extended to the Senior Fellows of the Institute, Elizabeth Abramowitz, Faustine Jones, and Samuel Wong for their many suggestions as the manuscript was written. The staffs of Howard University Library, Library of Congress, and the National Archives were especially helpful in providing research materials. I wish to extend my sincere thanks to the Institute's secretarial staff, Betty Fortune, Elaine Reed, and especially to Brenda Knight, who typed the manuscript in its various stages. Jane Midgley provided extremely valuable editorial assistance. Finally, I thank the following members of the Institute's research staff: Julius Hobson, Jr., John McClendon, and Herschelle Reed, who made substantial contributions in providing material for this study.

John E. Fleming
Washington, D.C.

July 1, 1976

FOREWORD

Affirmative action programs, which arose from the massive struggles of the Civil Rights Movement of the 1960s, are under attack in the 1970s. The country seems to be forgetting that the legacy of slavery—segregation, Jim Crowism, and racism—is still with us. Some critics feel that the federal government has gone too far in trying to secure equality and justice for blacks. Unsubstantiated charges have been made that the government is requiring employers to set quotas for the hiring of blacks, women, and other groups discriminated against. Evils and wrongs committed on the basis of race are unlikely to be remedied and corrected without taking race into account.

To act justly in the present and future, the past must be recalled because in large measure it shaped present conditions. The courage, resources, and commitment necessary to attain justice for blacks require that people of the current generation fully understand the pale shadow which the history of slavery, discrimination, and racism casts over the present. This is particularly important in analyzing the affirmative action concept and policies in higher education. Thus, the Institute for the Study of Educational Policy, through the research and writing of Dr. John Fleming, one of its Senior Fellows, has undertaken to lay before the public a chronicle of the black experience, especially as it relates to education.

Dr. Fleming's historical monograph chronicles two most important themes which vary only slightly throughout United States history. The first theme recounts the struggle and determination of blacks to acquire the education and knowledge which they felt were essential for them to acquire freedom, human dignity, and meaningful participation in the American society. The second theme is the denial of education and knowledge to blacks by those who were remorselessly determined to keep blacks slaves or second-class citizens. Very early it was recognized that the institution of slavery and the education of slaves were incompatible. Thus an overriding and enduring determination of blacks in their trek toward freedom and equality has been the pursuit of education and knowledge. The pursuit has not been undertaken to destroy the American Dream but to participate in it by making it a living reality for all, regardless of race, color, or creed. Those who have resisted this pursuit either deny that blacks are capable of benefiting from it or neglect the imperatives of black freedom, equality, dignity, and self-fulfillment.

Affirmative and aggressive action to secure the justice and equity blacks are entitled to has never worked against any substantial interest of other significant groups of Americans. For example, the public school system in the South got its real start with the enfranchisement of blacks, but it provided educational opportunity for poor whites as well. Blacks could only be kept in "their place" in the South by retarding the economic, social, and educational progress of the South generally. What was true of the South in the past is true of the entire nation today. The neglect of this country's great urban centers, where there are great concentrations of blacks, forebodes disaster not only for the cities but also for the country at large. Blacks may be regarded as a finger on the hand of America, as Booker T. Washington said. But a finger, if made gangrenous due to neglect and mistreatment, must be nourished and sustained or amputated to save the rest of the hand. The former course of action may be regarded as affirmative action; the latter is genocide.

The lengthening shadow of slavery can be shortened and eliminated. What is required is that America conscientiously and affirmatively move its ideals of equality, freedom, and justice toward the zenith. The Institute believes that by chronicling the facts of the black experience in education, the country will choose the bright light of noon over the lingering haze of a darkening twilight zone.

Kenneth S. Tollett
Chairman, National Advisory
Board
Institute for the Study of
Educational Policy

July, 1976

CONTENTS

PREFACE

This monograph chronicles selected events in the history of black people in America, from slavery to the present time, and examines certain key factors which impeded or enhanced their struggle to acquire an education. Needless to say, the barriers erected to keep blacks in ignorance, and thus in a state of submissiveness, were firmly established during slavery. Following the emancipation of the slaves, different, but no less effective, impediments were institutionalized to prevent them from acquiring quality education and breaking out of the caste system designed for them at the turn of the nineteenth century.

This study was undertaken because racism has been institutionalized, and many of the historical problems for, and barriers to, blacks acquiring an education remain with us today. Further, it became more and more evident that the federal government, as well as the nation, began to waver in its commitment to equality of opportunity for black Americans. This reassessment of the placement of black people in American society is reminiscent of the short-lived effort to compensate them during the era of Reconstruction, which followed the Civil War more than a century ago. One present-day manifestation of retrenchment is the current attack on, and hostility toward, affirmative action.

The concept of affirmative action was developed during the 1960s when blacks, women, and other minorities were extremely vocal in their demands for equal rights and equal justice. This demand was stimulated in 1954 when the United States Supreme Court, in the now famous *Brown* decision, provided the legal basis for the destruction of segregation. In the next decade, beginning with the Montgomery, Alabama bus boycott and the emergence of Dr. Martin Luther King, Jr., as a powerful civil rights leader, the struggles for racial equality in the South received the attention of the entire nation. By 1960, when student demonstrations became a decisive tool for desegregation, the nation had witnessed the horror of beatings, harrassment, cattle prods, bombings, and other forms of violence directed at those who worked peacefully for equal rights. And in 1964, protests and demonstrations had spread throughout even the northern urban centers.

This decade of civil rights activity caused the nation to reexamine its commitment to racial equality, but it was obvious that both legal action and direct action were of limited usefulness. What was needed was a solid and unambiguous commitment, by the federal government and U.S. citizens, to desegregate and to provide equality in hiring, housing, education, and a higher standard of living for blacks in the country. The riots in major cities throughout the United States in 1968 after the death of Martin Luther King, Jr., demonstrated that no substantial effort had been made to alleviate racial inequality.

President Lyndon B. Johnson recognized the extent of the problem in 1965 when he issued his Executive Order 11246, an order designed to eradicate systemic discrimination through the incorporation of affirmative action requirements in the government's contract compliance program. According to the executive order's implementing regulations, government contractors are required to identify and then eliminate all discriminatory practices based upon race and sex. Further, the affirmative action obligation required that contractors take additional steps designed to overcome vestiges of systemic discrimination. As affirmative action programs achieved results, they came under increasing attack—attacks often led by members of the academic community.

The attacks on affirmative action programs as they relate to institutions of higher education are all the more momentous because those programs are the key to the future advancement of black people. Through the acquisition of an education, blacks can obtain better jobs and houses, and improve their economic situation in line with the rest of American society. This book narrates the historical struggle of blacks and serves as a reminder to the larger society of blacks' continued deprivation. Finally, this historical analysis pointedly illustrates that a sustained commitment to affirmative action is necessary to rectify generations of denial.

THE LENGTHENING
SHADOW OF SLAVERY

BLACK EFFORTS TO ACQUIRE AN EDUCATION DURING THE AGE OF SLAVERY

The introduction of slavery into the New World was primarily motivated by a shortage of labor and an overabundance of land. Although North America was settled by Europeans from a feudal society, chattel slavery was foreign to European, especially English, customs and laws. Therefore, as the English colonies moved from a reliance on indentured servitude to the enslavement of African peoples, an elaborate system of philosophical and legal supports was developed to justify human bondage. As the economic institution of slavery became more complex, the rationale and legal system which maintained slavery also increased in complexity. The result was that slavery developed into more than a system of labor; the peculiar institution became the cornerstone of southern society.

The institution of slavery was dependent upon keeping the enslaved in a state of ignorance; for knowledge was the one factor which could have destroyed it. A labyrinth of philosophical arguments, based upon the alleged inferiority of black people, was used to justify their enslavement, and a highly developed legal system was used to deny them an education. Their lack of education, in turn, was used to justify and perpetuate slavery.

In spite of the complex system of barriers erected to prevent blacks from acquiring an education, a few managed to obtain varying degrees of literacy. Within the slave system, a few whites were willing to break the slave codes to teach a favorite slave, who was often a relative, to read and write. Religious instruction often encouraged a slave to learn to read the Bible. The economics of plantation life necessitated teaching certain slaves skills and crafts, and, of course, there were the slaves who were self-taught.

Free blacks did not fare much better than the slaves. As it became apparent that their existence in a slave society was a threat, they were prohibited from learning to read and write, and their lives became more and more circumscribed. Free blacks in the North were given few opportunities to attend schools. Race prejudice and discrimination caused northern whites to segregate blacks into inferior schools—if schools were provided at all. Only through their initiative and the assistance of abolitionists were some blacks able to overcome the barriers and acquire a degree of learning.

But those who did were the exceptions. By the end of the Civil War it was readily apparent that the society as a whole, North and South, had successfully kept the majority of 4.5 million blacks illiterate.

JUSTIFICATION FOR THE ENSLAVEMENT OF BLACK PEOPLE
Economic Foundation of Slavery

Much work remains to be done on the economic history of Afro-Americans. While monographs have been written on various aspects of the economic plight of black people, a comprehensive historical analysis of the black economic situation within the general economy has not been made. Although, by no means comprehensive, this monograph, in part, will illustrate how the present pressing problems of blacks are tied to the American economy—a situation which has existed from the earliest date of the institution of slavery to the present. The economic exploitation of blacks during slavery is more readily apparent than the present day exploitation which is evident in systemic racism.

The basis for European settlement of the North American continent has been obscured by the emphasis given to the search for religious and civil rights. But whites who settled on Indian territory on the North American continent were aided in their venture by powerful economic interests. The Dutch West Indies Company, which transported Europeans to the New World, wished to exploit the labor of the immigrants. The efforts to transplant

European feudalism to American soil failed because the New World, unlike Europe, offered an abundance of free land. Thus, the early settlers could not be bound to the soil.[1]

The necessity to provide an alternative labor force to the feudal system led to the development of indentured servitude. In exchange for passage across the Atlantic Ocean, a person agreed to work for a stipulated number of years. This system was especially influential in shaping the character of the labor force of early colonial America. Early black arrivals in English-speaking America were put under this system of indentured servitude which existed throughout all the colonies. The Puritans indentured whites, blacks and Indians. While certain indentured servants were forced into lifetime service, paving the way for the introduction of slavery, the effort to enslave the native population failed, among other reasons, because their knowledge of the terrain enabled them to successfully escape bondage.[2]

While the institution of slavery was developing in other colonies, slavery was prohibited in Georgia when it was first established as a colony in 1732. The reason was twofold. On the one hand, the colony was to provide a place for persecuted Protestants, paupers, and unlawful elements, and they in turn would be the work force; on the other hand, Georgia was to serve as a buffer between the colony of South Carolina and Spanish Florida and thus inhibit fugitive slaves who wanted to join the Indians on the frontier. However, Georgia's white population was insufficient to meet the labor demands, and slavery became necessary despite problems of runaway slaves from slaveholders.[3]

As the system of perpetual bondage developed, there was also an attempt to enslave whites. Whites proved unsuitable for slavery because they ran away too, but because of their skin color could easily assimilate into the population. Social pressure was also brought to bear on those who enslaved whites because of the moral and ethical implications of white slavery. All facts considered, then, the African proved to be the most suitable for slavery. Unlike the Indian, he was foreign to America and had a historical background in agriculture. But more important, his physical appearance was distinctively different from whites. This distinction provided the root of the racist ideological rationale formulated to justify black enslavement.[4]

With the emergence of African slavery, white servitude declined. Slavery gave the colonial labor system its essential stability, and all slaves were controlled by whites. As the supply of indentured servants diminished, thereby becoming too inefficient and costly, slaves increasingly filled the demand for labor. In New York in 1626, the Dutch West Indies Company

imported slaves when unable to get Europeans to stay permanently.
Slaves worked on farms, public buildings, and did military work in place of free
workers. The very survival of this colony would have been doubtful except
for slavery. Slave labor ultimately transformed the colony from a shaky
commercial venture into a permanent settlement. Boston traders, who were
involved in the triangular trade and who had earlier gotten slaves from the
West Indies, began to import them from Africa. Trade was becoming an
international activity. The Dutch West Indies Company and the English
Royal African Company were backed by their respective governments and
armed forces to gain hegemony in the slave trade. Despite these difficulties,
and the fact that New England merchants were forced to import slaves from
distant West Africa, slavery still proved profitable. However, when slavery is
examined within the larger context of the total colonial society, slavery was of
greater economic importance to the southern colonies than any other region of
colonial America.[5]

Harold D. Woodman found, in *Slavery and the Southern Economy*, that

> by the end of the seventeenth century, the 28,000 Negroes—most of
> them slaves—who lived in the southern colonies were already a more
> important source of labor than the indentured whites. Ownership of
> Negro slaves seemed to have many obvious advantages in this place of
> high wages and relatively cheap land . . . The number of Negro slaves
> increased rapidly in the eighteenth century. By 1780 more than a half a
> million slaves lived in the United States, 90% of them in the South.[6]

African slavery benefited the colonial economies as well as British
trading interests. During the eighteenth century, sugar was the predominant
commodity in international trade, and consequently the commercial activities
of the North American colonies were of secondary importance. While the
mercantile-colonial policies of Britain stifled the efforts to expand North
American commerce, Britain encouraged the colonies to participate in the
triangular slave trade, further establishing the system of slavery in America.[7]

As northern colonies began more and more to diversify, the need for
slave labor decreased. Nevertheless, commercial interest, especially in the
New England colonies, contributed to the entrenchment of slavery in the
southern colonies. New Englanders actively engaged in the triangular slave
trade and made great profits at the expense of human suffering. Slave trading
ships from Massachusetts, Rhode Island, Connecticut, and to a lesser degree
from New Hampshire, engaged early in the trade, which continued largely
unabated until the Revolution. The trade was principally responsible for the

commercial rise of Newport. Slaves were purchased and taken to South Carolina in exchange for ship-building stores or to the West Indies in exchange for molasses, which was made into rum and shipped to Africa for more slaves.[8] Thus, New England prospered economically at the expense of the human rights of black people.

Although the southern climate—hot summers and long growing seasons—and its rich soil and navigable rivers may have facilitated the growth of agriculture (more specifically, the plantation system of growing staple crops), the decision to rely on slave labor in agricultural pursuits was a deliberate choice. This choice was motivated primarily by economic incentives: men reasoned that a greater return on their investments could be secured through the use of slave labor. Through the labor and sweat of others, the new masters hoped to become wealthy men.[9] Whatever other motives existed for the enslavement of Africans, the primary motive was economic. Many other arguments were used to justify and perpetuate an economic system that benefited a small, select number of whites.

Not until after the American Revolution was the South to realize just how profitable slavery could be. During the seventeenth century, the black population in the South increased slowly, and southern landholders relied chiefly upon white labor during this period. Only after the English and colonial merchants began trading in slaves did Africans arrive in the South in large numbers. By the beginning of the American Revolution, blacks and whites were evenly divided in Virginia's population; further south in South Carolina, blacks outnumbered whites two to one.[10] Still, it was not until after the Revolution, and the establishment of a new nation, that slavery came into its own.

The Philosophical Arguments

The basic motive for the institution of chattel slavery in America was economic, but slavery, contrary to English tradition, had to be justified on grounds other than economic necessity. Therefore, over a period of years an elaborate system of philosophical justifications for slavery developed, as southerners used the arguments of the Greeks and Romans, who thought that slavery was logical and conformed to the natural order of things. Building upon the Christian sanction of slavery and other arguments down to the seventeenth century, southerners moved from an initial casual defense in the late eighteenth century to a studied rebuttal of anti-slavery arguments as the nation prepared for Civil War.[11]

Intertwined with the arguments for slavery was the issue of slave education, which appeared early during the colonial period. Support for limited black instruction came from the very people who also supported slavery. The seventeenth century established church accepted the reality of black slavery and white supremacy, but desired to assure that the relationship worked to the mutual benefit of both slaves and masters. The church impressed upon the masters their duty to afford the slaves the opportunity for salvation and, at the same time, emphasized the duty of the slaves to obey their masters.[12]

The movement to provide religious instruction to the slaves gained more acceptance in the North with such religious leaders as Cotton Mather, who founded a school for teaching slaves. In the South, this argument met with serious objections from slaveholders, for most believed that blacks were of a different species from white men: since they had no souls, Christianity could not benefit them. What is more, they did not want the slaves to receive the sacraments because the administration of the sacraments would have elevated them and dissolved their status as slaves.[13] Thus, before the revolutionary war, the arguments used to justify slavery precluded the slaves from acquiring an education even through religious instruction or activities.

During the revolutionary war period, for a fleeting moment, some thought to extend the natural rights philosophy to the slaves. The Virginian Thomas Jefferson went so far as to list slavery and the slave code as a grievance against Great Britain in his first draft of the Declaration of Independence, a provision later struck out by his fellow southerners. Also, many white Americans were hard-pressed to justify slavery at a time when thousands of blacks were fighting for the freedom of the Americans colonies. Some authors even go so far as to suggest that blacks were the true freedom fighters—fighting for and against the British, depending upon what side offered the best hopes of personal freedom.[14]

The period from 1790 to 1820 marked a state of quiescence in the pro-slavery arguments. The ideals of the revolutionary period had much influence in the North, but little in the South. Most southerners throughout the period favored slavery. This attitude was reinforced by dramatic events which occurred over the succeeding decades. The heated debates in Congress over the Missouri Compromise are said to have had a direct influence on Denmark Vesey's planned insurrection in Charleston, South Carolina in 1822. Vesey, a freed slave who could read and write, was an anomaly in southern society. Nat Turner's rebellion in Southhampton, Virginia, sent terror throughout the

South. David Walker's *Appeal to the Colored Citizens of the World,* written by a black man from the South who later migrated North, caused slaveholders not only to defend slavery, but also to deny what little educational opportunities a slave or free man was able to achieve in what had previously been a relatively open society.[15] These events and developments, in addition to the rise of the Abolitionists, who became more and more dedicated to the destruction of slavery, aroused southerners to a vehement defense of slavery.

Because southerners felt slavery was in imminent danger, the institution itself was systematically defended as of mutual benefit to black and white. Without apology, the South presented its case to the world. Slavery was reexamined from the angles of natural and social history, ethnology, allied sciences, political and social sciences, and of course the Scripture. Some of the best thinkers in the South lent their support. John C. Calhoun was one of the early leading exponents of the theory that slavery was a positive good. Other exponents included the political economist Professor Thomas R. Dew; the social philosopher George Fitzhugh, the Baptist minister Thornton Stringfellow; and the scientist Dr. Samuel Cartwright. These and other writers examined slavery from all perspectives.[16]

Slavery was viewed not as a moral evil to be tolerated, but as a positive good for both slave and slaveholder. The Bible was used to provide the most systematic statement on slavery, from the curse of Cain in Genesis to the exhortation of the Apostles that slaves should obey their masters. While the church in the South condoned slavery, it attempted to regulate the slave-master relationship by encouraging masters to deal justly with their slaves and for slaves to obey their masters. The religious exponents of slavery believed that blacks were slaves as a result of their sins. The leading "scientists" proposed that slavery was a result of black inferiority. Southern ethnologists tried to hypothesize that blacks were different, and tried to point out the physical and mental differences to support the supposition that different social endowments gave blacks more animal qualities. They were said to be able to imitate behavior but could never be inventive, a reflection of higher mental qualities.[17]

Since the pro-slavery arguments projected the Negro as being simply inferior, belonging to another species entirely, it was promulgated in theory that the Negro could not be trained beyond fulfilling the elementary functions required of slave life. Planters discouraged religious instruction because they feared that the slave would become discontent, but as soon as the various churches expressed support for the institution of slavery, some of the animosity toward black religious instruction subsided.[18]

Slave revolts and abolitionist pressure not only encouraged southerners to rise to the defense of slavery, but also made southerners more diligent in their efforts to protect the institution and their southern society. State legislatures barred the teaching of reading and writing to slaves, and those states with laws already on the books passed measures to encourage stricter enforcement (see the section on the slave codes).[19]

The little education that was provided in the South was designed to reinforce the slaves' feeling of inferiority and to make them content with their position in the social order. They were told that Africans were barbarians and had no history prior to the coming of Europeans. The destruction of African history was imperative if the systematic attempt to brainwash them was to succeed. Africans were brought to the United States to serve the labor needs of their masters, and their education was geared accordingly. Most whites believed that blacks could not acquire a formal education, and those who believed they could feared that cultivated minds would arouse defiance in blacks.[20]

Fear of slave revolts was the primary reason for the development of a legal system to regiment the life of the slave and to protect southern society. Southerners knew the importance of rationalizing slavery and developing an intellectual commitment to, and defense of, slavery, but even more basic was the legal justification of the institution.

The Legal Basis for Slavery

Little is known of the status of the first blacks who arrived in the English settlement in North America. Yet, within fifty years, slavery and a well-developed legal system to justify the institution of slavery were commonplace in Maryland and Virginia. Since slavery ran counter to English law and tradition, the colonists had to justify the institution by emphasizing such differences as color, religion, and life style between themselves and Africans. As early as 1640, the general court in Virginia made a distinction between white and black runaway servants, sentencing the two whites to additional years in service, while sentencing the lone black to service for life. Further distinctions were made: the colonists outlawed miscegenation and barred all types of·sexual union between the two races.[21]

The concept that one man could hold another man as property had no basis in the traditional sense of English concepts and legal categories. Africans were declared to be either real or personal property (chattel), according to the legal needs of the colonies. Once it had been established in practice and law that blacks were to be held in involuntary servitude, it was necessary to maintain a system of laws to regulate the behavior of slaves. Initially, the laws were aimed at solving particular problems arising out of slavery, but they were later codified and became known as the slave codes. This system grew slowly in the older states, but newer slave states, such as Georgia, readily adopted the pattern established by older states like South Carolina. Except in those instances in which acts were passed in panic situations, the punishment prescribed in the slave codes in the North was generally lighter than that in the South. The codes in the South varied in detail, but retained basic underlying similarities.[22]

South Carolina is a prime example of a state that had developed an elaborate slave code. By the beginning of the eighteenth century, slaves outnumbered whites in the colony, which made the whites fearful of slave insurrections. This fear became reality during the 1730s, when a series of uprisings culminated in the Stono River Rebellion of 1739. A group of slaves attacked a warehouse, killed two guards and appropriated arms and powder, in an area about twenty miles southwest of Charleston at Stono. The band proceeded south toward St. Augustine where they hoped to join the Spanish in Florida. The rebels' ranks enlarged to seventy-five or eighty as they burned their way south. Before the insurgents were able to succeed with their plan, they were overcome by the militia. Some escaped; most were killed, but not before they had killed an estimated twenty-five whites.[23]

Following the suppression of the rebellion, South Carolina responded immediately with oppressive legislation. On May 10, 1740, the legislature passed "An Act for the Better Ordering and Governing of Negroes and Other Slaves in this Province." The law was a comprehensive attempt to govern nearly all aspects of slave life. Slaves were declared "absolute slaves," while the status of black children was determined by the status of their mothers. Strict travel restrictions were enforced. Slaves had to submit to the interrogation of any white or face death for refusal. They were denied the right to use firearms, deal in commerce, operate boats, beat drums, and drink or sell liquor. Their masters had complete control over them. Slaves convicted of either assaulting a white person or raping a white woman received the death penalty. The code went so far as to prescribe the type of cloth slaves were to be given, and, of course, they were denied any form of education.[24]

Most state legislators quickly responded to the needs of the planter class and approved additional legislation to regulate the slaves. Virginia passed an ordinance declaring that baptism of a slave does not alter his condition of bondage. Most states also passed laws aimed at preventing slave runaways. Even the North—Connecticut, for example—passed such an act as early as 1715.[25]

The development of the slave code was impeded during the revolutionary and early nationalist periods. As Americans realized, prior to the revolutionary war, that they were no longer Englishmen, they also grew conscious of their own prejudice against blacks. Some began to question the institution of slavery. Others even asserted the fundamental equality of black men with white men. Much of this movement was led by Quakers who, decades before the war, had concluded that slavery was wrong.[26]

Of the black man's participation in the war effort, Benjamin Quarles said:

> In the Revolutionary War the American Negro was a participant and a symbol. He was active on the battlefronts and behind the lines; in his expectations and in the gains he registered during the war, he personified the goal of that freedom in whose name the struggle was waged. The Negro's role in the Revolution can best be understood by realizing that his major loyalty was not to a place nor to a people, but to a principle. Insofar as he had freedom of choice, he was likely to join the side that made him the quickest and best offer in terms of those "unalienable rights" of which Mr. Jefferson has spoken. Whoever invoked the image of liberty, be he American or British, could count on a ready response from the blacks.[27]

After fighting valiantly for both sides in the name of freedom, blacks scarcely improved their lot. Some of those who embraced the Loyalists or British subjects remained slaves; others were shipped to the West Indies, Canada, England, and Europe, where many encountered difficulty securing the land grants promised. Blacks who remained in America were equally disillusioned. The condition of the slaves was unchanged. Nevertheless, a number of blacks had gained their freedom, and the national commitment to the principles of liberty and equality provided some support for the growing abolitionist movement.[28]

After realizing the shortcomings of the Articles of Confederation, the victorious Americans finally adopted a permanent constitution in which there is no mention of black Americans. Article I, Section 2 specified "all other persons," meaning slaves, were to be counted as three-fifths of a person in determining state representation; Section 9 of the same article prohibited the federal government from interfering with the importation of slaves until 1808; and Article IV, Section 2 provided for the return of fugitive slaves.[29]

The completed Constitution was designed to protect slavery where it existed. The compromise pleased southerners and those who did not want to formally recognize slavery in a document which represented the fundamental law of the land. Having fought a war on the grounds that all men were created equal, the founding fathers were hard-pressed to recognize slavery. The Constitution defined the slave both as a man and property, but his status as an American was not defined until after the Civil War.[30] Meanwhile, it was left to the individual states to determine the status of slaves.

THE NATIONAL PERIOD

The Consolidation of Slavery as an Economic Institution After the Revolutionary War

Britain's restrictive legislation, designed to carry out its mercantilist policies, resulted in a depression which lasted from 1763 to 1770. Events quickly led to war and subsequent American freedom, but independence and the end of restrictions did not lead to immediate prosperity. Besides shortages of manufactured goods and property damages from the war, there was also economic inflation—the product of expansion of colonial paper money.[31]

It has been noted how revolutionary zeal led to a questioning of slavery and the assertion that the ideas of equality and the rights of man should be extended to the Negro. But even more significant for slavery in the South was the sluggish southern economy. The South not only suffered the economic plight of the nation as a whole, but also the region had its own particular economic problems. The most important difficulty was the decline in the price of tobacco. This was the foremost economic problem because tobacco was the leading staple in the South and remained so up to the beginning of the nineteenth century.[32]

The prospects of substituting rice and indigo as alternative staple crops were slim; rice could be grown in few places and indigo was unprofitable because of the British withdrawal of its bounties. As pointed out, the legal position of enslaved blacks had been firmly established by 1790—yet the numerous difficulties of the South's economy, especially those of the older tobacco states, due to the drop in prices, gave rise to scattered cries to end slavery. Virginia, which had been the leading producer of tobacco, was faced with an even greater problem as the fertility of the soil degenerated rapidly, making it difficult to run plantations on a profitable basis. Both George Washington and James Madison were confronted with this dilemma. Some entertained the idea of abandoning plantation production of single staple crops and of broadening the variety of farm produce. However, the existence of a large unproductive slave labor force was considered dangerous, and this led some southerners to propose the colonization of blacks.[33]

In Virginia in 1800, the size of the black population caused considerable alarm. There was a growing fear of slave revolts encouraged by free blacks who were considered especially undesirable. This, coupled with the decreased production of tobacco, led to a brief interest in black colonization. (For a more detailed discussion see the section on colonization.) The crisis in production was followed by the invention of the cotton gin which had a major consequence for slavery in general and the education of blacks in particular.[34]

A number of discoveries had revolutionized the British textile industry, and the production of cotton soon became the leading southern export commodity. The South faced the dilemma of a decrease in demand for its traditional export staples while maintaining its heavy investment in slaves. Thus, the invention of the cotton gin can be viewed as a response to the dilemma rather than as an independent accident. Consequently, the rapid acceleration in demand for cotton revitalized the peculiar institution of slavery.[35]

The British demand for cotton was extremely high. Britain imported a million pounds of cotton in the first half of the eighteenth century, which increased to 56 million by 1800. The traditional sources of the supply—the West Indies, Isles of Bourbon, The Levant, and Brazil—could not meet the demand, which afforded the southern states an opportunity to increase their production for export. Since the cotton gin was cheap to reproduce, it became widely available.[36]

Ironically, the first cotton gin in the state of Mississippi was built by a slave mechanic named Barclay, who used a drawing of Eli Whitney's gin to build one in 1795, and Mississippi, along with other states, substantially increased cotton production. This was in response to the rise in cotton prices from 1815 to 1824. In 1821, for example, some twenty thousand bales were grown in Mississippi. The introduction of cotton as the main commodity in southern slavery further limited black people's chances for an education.[37]

This discussion of slavery has centered on the economic reasons for its derivation, existence, entrenchment, and justification. Attention now will turn to changes in the legal restrictions placed on the slaves following the revolutionary war.

Legal Restrictions During the National Period

The nature of the slave system as defined by the slave codes differed little in the national period from what it was in the colonial era, except that laws were often harsher; slaves were defined as property and subject to cruel and inhuman treatment. Generally, masters had complete control over their slaves, but most states placed a limit on punishment that would endanger life and limb. The codes regulated criminal acts and sanctioned more severe punishment for blacks than that prescribed for whites. Those convicted of rebellion were subject to the death penalty. Even those whites who were convicted of inciting slaves to rebel were subject to the death penalty.[38]

Special laws needed to monitor the slave's already circumscribed existence were proposed, legitimized, and rigorously enforced. This practice continued throughout the period of slavery in the United States. The refusal to allow slaves to engage in trade eliminated them from economic competition with whites. These and other prohibitions were enforced by slave patrols. The code also regulated the internal slave trade and the manumission of slaves. As time progressed, emancipation was generally prohibited throughout the South. There were also laws to protect the slaves, but these laws were especially designed to protect the slaves' value as property rather than as persons.[39]

The laws which comprised the slave code were based on the alleged inferiority of black people and were designed to protect the institution of slavery. The daily routine of a slave's world was designed in such a manner as to discourage those slaves who wished to acquire an education. Although there were a few white slave owners who desired, for various reasons, to teach their slaves how to read and write, most southerners reasoned that "teaching may easily awaken independent ideas in the minds of the pupil." Therefore, many state officials acted to protect themselves against rebellion and conspiracy by keeping Negroes in ignorance.[40]

This fear of enlightened slaves who might cause others to rebel was evident throughout the South. In 1800, South Carolina reenacted a law banning "slaves, free Negroes, mulattoes, and mestizos" from being taught to read and write. Virginia in 1819 prescribed corporal punishment, not exceeding twenty lashes, for any slaves assembling to read and write. North Carolina's ban against slave education included a punishment of thirty-nine lashes for a free Negro, and a $200 fine for a white caught teaching a slave to read and write and providing him with any sort of literature—the Bible not excepted. In Georgia, the fine for a white teaching a free Negro or slave to

write was $500 and imprisonment at the discretion of the court. This particu-
lar law, enacted in 1829, even banned a father teaching his own child. In
Louisiana, a prison term of one year was provided for anyone convicted of
teaching slaves.[41]

Although southern states passed laws prohibiting slaves from obtaining
an education, enforcement of the laws was another matter, at least up to the
1830s when the course of events led to a more stringent enforcement of the
slave codes. The Abolitionists stepped up their attack on slavery and bom-
barded the South with antislavery literature. One of the most devastating
attacks on slavery was written by David Walker, born in North Carolina in
1785. Walker was the son of a slave father and a free mother. Little is known
of his early life, except that he somehow acquired an education, a monumental feat in itself. Repelled by slavery and the fate of the free Negro, Walker left
the South and settled in Boston. In September 1829, he issued his *Appeal to
the Coloured Citizens of the World,* in which he lamented the evils of slavery
and called upon the nation to repent of its sin or face destruction. The *Appeal*
created an uproar throughout the South. Men still remembered the planned
insurrection of Denmark Vesey, who also had been free and could read and
write. Georgia and Louisiana passed laws providing the death penalty for the
circulation of abolitionist material among slaves. North Carolina made it a
criminal offense to teach a slave to read.[42]

Yet, the most devastating barrier to black education came in the wake of
Nat Turner's rebellion. Turner, born October 2, 1800, probably lived all of
his life in Southhampton, Virginia. Turner had learned how to read, and
when time permitted, he read from the Bible, which led to his belief that he
had been ordained to accomplish a great mission in life. This mission was to
strike a blow for liberty. After the rebellion had been contained, numerous
innocent blacks were murdered out of fear and in retaliation for those whites
Turner killed during the insurrection.[43]

The South reacted. Virginia prohibited all meetings in which Negroes
and slaves were taught to read and write. This ban extended to both black and
white. The state legislators further prohibited slaves and free Negroes from
preaching, and slaves from attending services held by white preachers without special permission. A complete ban was placed on all publications urging
persons to rebel.[44] A member of the Virginia House of Delegates said in 1832:

> We have, as far as possible, closed every avenue by which light might
> enter their [the slaves] minds. If we could extinguish the capacity to see
> the light, our work would be completed; they would then be on a level
> with the beasts of the field, and we should be safe![45]

Similar actions, as in Virginia, occurred in other parts of the South. Enforcement was so stringent in North Carolina that the slave patrols were ordered to search all of the free blacks' houses for books or publications of any kind.[46]

The slave codes thus effectively served to restrict severely or eliminate the slaves' efforts to become educated. But even this was not deemed sufficient for the suppression of either slave or free black people. The climax came in the *Dred Scott* decision of 1857. Since the case is well known, the basic decision will be presented here.

The Supreme Court held in its decision that the Constitution contained implicit distinctions between white citizens and Negroes, as far as the exercise of constitutional rights was concerned. Whites were born with certain rights, while blacks had only those rights that whites were willing to extend to them. The Constitution was made by and for whites; persons of African descent, whether slave or free, were not included as part of the people. Free Negroes were not protected by the Constitution and certainly not slaves, who were merely property under the entire control of the slave states. Not until passage of the Thirteenth, Fourteenth, and Fifteenth Amendments were these obstructions removed and the *Dred Scott* decision overturned.[47]

Thus, the system of slavery, reinforced by slave codes, explicitly prohibited blacks from learning how to read and write. Since northern states outlawed slavery during the early nationalist period, the question remained: to what extent were free northern blacks offered opportunities for equality in American society? Was freedom alone enough to facilitate black education or were barriers, similar to the slave codes, erected to prevent free blacks from acquiring an education prior to the Civil War? These and other questions are discussed in the following section on legal restrictions on free blacks.

Legal Restrictions Against Free Blacks in the North and South Prior to 1865

After the Revolution the federal government, as well as the individual states, defined separately what constituted the legal status of free blacks. The states generally excluded them from holding state citizenship, while the Constitution was silent on the matter, having made no mention of color or race. Yet, both state and federal governments generally agreed prior to the Civil War that blacks were inferior and their legal status should reflect this. The dominant race held that blacks, whether slave or free, could never achieve equality in the United States.[48]

The policies of the federal government were soon reflected in legislation passed by Congress. In 1790, Congress limited naturalization to white aliens.

In 1810, blacks were prohibited from carrying the United States mail. In addition to these examples of discriminatory legislation, Congress repeatedly admitted new states into the Union whose constitutions placed severe restrictions on the rights of free Negroes. Congress banned blacks from service in the militia, but took no action regarding their service in the Army, Navy, and Marines. Thus Congress, by default, gave blacks the opportunity to accumulate a long history of distinguished service in the armed forces.[49]

In spite of restrictive federal legislation, free blacks continued their uphill battle for political equality. In 1800, the Reverend Absolom Jones of Philadelphia headed a group of blacks who petitioned Congress to correct the evils of the African slave trade and, careful not to call for an immediate end to slavery, politely asked that the peculiar institution gradually be abolished. Congressmen exploded at the nerve of these free blacks who had the audacity to use a constitutional right of petition for redress of grievances. Many felt that the petition should not be honored by taking action of any sort. Others feared that lack of action would encourage them to seek fuller participation in the democratic process. Having denied them nearly all opportunity for education, some lawmakers illogically proceeded to attack the petition on the basis that some of the petitioners could not write their names and had to sign with their mark. Congress disposed of the issue by voting to refuse to consider the question of domestic slavery.[50]

During the 1820-1821 debates on the admission of Missouri to the Union, the legal status of free Negroes was raised once again. Missouri's constitution included provisions which guaranteed its citizens the right to own slaves, and also instructed the state legislature to enact the necessary legislation to ban free Negroes from entering the state for any reason. Missourians reasoned that every state barred blacks from voting, giving evidence in court, and marrying white persons, while no state permitted them to join the militia. A compromise was reached and Missouri was admitted to the Union on condition of a vague clause which stated that the constitutional provision in question would not be used to exclude the enjoyment of any privileges and immunities of United States citizens. The final resolution on the status of free Negroes before the war was thus postponed until a decision was reached in the *Dred Scott* case.[51]

The rise of Andrew Jackson to prominence and the subsequent expansion of white male suffrage did not enhance the political position of free blacks. In fact, often the broadening of the franchise was done at their expense. Only five states—Massachusetts, Rhode Island, New Hampshire, Vermont, and Maine—permitted Negroes to vote with whites by 1860. Many whites feared that if universal manhood suffrage was extended, then blacks not only would control their political wards in the ghettos, but would also hold the balance of power in close political contests and thus be in a position to bargain successfully for their rights. Since it was generally felt that blacks were inferior and not entitled to the same treatment as whites, it was deemed best to exclude blacks altogether from the polls. Those who argued in favor of suffrage for black men feared that their exclusion would pose a precedent for the exclusion of men from other minority groups.[52]

At the federal level prior to the Civil War, the question of the legal status of free blacks was settled by the *Dred Scott* case, but the decision also had far-reaching implications for free Negroes. The Court ruled that Dred Scott was not a citizen because he was a slave. According to Chief Justice Taney, no Negro, slave or free, could be a citizen. Regardless of action taken by individual states in bestowing political rights on free Negroes, the Constitution reserved to Congress the right of conferring citizenship, and it could not be conferred by a state.[53] The question concerning the status of blacks was settled after the Civil War when Congress adopted, and the states passed, the Fourteenth Amendment to the Constitution.

As the Civil War approached, the legal status of free Negroes both in the North and South had deteriorated considerably. Theoretically, there were some state provisions for the legal protection of blacks, but even those were qualified. Often, where free blacks were permitted to testify in court, they were prohibited from testifying against whites; this meant, in effect, that a white man could literally murder a black and get away with it if witnessed by another black person only. Other northern states forbade blacks from owning real estate, making contracts, and filing law suits. Blacks were either excluded from railroads cars, stagecoaches, and steamboats or assigned to special sections. When permitted, they were forced to sit in remote corners of theaters and lecture halls; they could not enter most hotels and restaurants, and when permitted in white churches, were assigned to "Negro pews." They were treated in segregated hospitals, "educated" in segregated schools, jailed in segregated prisons, and buried in segregated cemeteries. Where no statute regulated their behavior, custom and practice excluded them; thus, what was not accomplished by law was accomplished through extralegal methods. In 1829 mob action in Cincinnati, for example, forced more than half of that city's blacks to leave. Between 1832 and 1849, five major anti-Negro riots occurred in Philadelphia. In 1834 a white mob stormed the Negro section of town and destroyed homes, churches, and meeting halls and forced hundreds to flee.[54]

Conditions for the free people of color in the South were even more deplorable since their very presence was an anomaly in a slaveholding society and a threat, whether actual or perceived, to the slave system. In addition to the serious legal restrictions imposed on the southern free blacks, they were subject even more to the capricious whims of the white population. They faced the very real possibility of losing their freedom if, at any time, they could not prove that they were indeed free. The slave codes, promulgated ostensibly for the slaves, often included provisions governing free blacks; and even when this was not the case, the codes themselves were often used to govern the behavior of free blacks.[55]

Thus, the entire legal system as it related to free blacks, whether federal or state, North or South, was based on the alleged inferiority of blacks. The effect on the efforts of black people to acquire an education was catastrophic. In light of the legal barriers, it is a wonder that any blacks at all managed to obtain a degree of literacy prior to the Civil War.

THE EDUCATION OF BLACKS DURING THE AGE OF SLAVERY

Slaves: Their Quest for Education

The very nature of the slave system prevented the vast majority of blacks from acquiring the traditional forms of education. Frederick Douglass reasoned that slaveholders refused to educate their slaves because to do so would make the slaves discontented and provide them with the tools to gain their freedom. Since the master's object was to maintain complete control and optimum production, there was constant vigilance against slaves learning.[56]

Most slaves lived in rural areas on plantations least conducive to learning even through the "hidden passage."* The medium-to-large plantations were located in the Black Belt areas of Louisiana, Mississippi, Alabama, and the rice swamps and sea islands of South Carolina and Georgia. Less than 10 percent of all slaves lived in what could be classified as urban areas. Although Virginia had more slaves than any other single state, the majority of slaves lived throughout the deep South.[57]

Whereas the majority of slaveholding units were small, the majority of

---

* The "hidden passage" was the means by which slaves were able to gain knowledge and a degree of literacy in spite of the restrictions of the slave system. This occurred through a variety of means which included listening to the conversations of whites, "borrowing" books and teaching oneself to read, receiving religious instruction, and even operating clandestine slave "schools."

slaves—in terms of numbers—lived on larger units. Thus, most slaves never had the opportunity for close association with slaveholders which those on the smaller farms had. Here, the farmers were forced to work side by side with their slaves. Notwithstanding this close association, farms were too small to allow a division of labor; there was little opportunity to gain a measure of skills. In contrast, the larger plantations, those with thirty or more slaves, had increased efficiency and specialization. There was a clear distinction between household and field hands. On the larger plantations jobs were divided into such categories as livestock care, driving wagons, caring for vegetables, and skilled artisans, which will be discussed separately.[58]

Of course, the slaves' day varied from plantation to plantation depending on the type of crop grown and the season of the year. Nevertheless, there were some common features. The slave rose before sunrise to prepare his meal for work in the field, where he remained until dusk. To assure that the slave's labor was fully utilized, indoor tasks were saved for inclement weather. Even children were usually put to work by the age of five or six. They followed their mothers to the field to tote water and to perform whatever other tasks they could. Although older slaves were generally spared field work, they were still expected to be productive in other forms of work; even disabled slaves were employed as spinners.[59] Thus, as has been shown, the legal system prohibited slave education, while the economic system of slavery was established for efficiency in production which precluded opportunities for traditional forms of learning.

Yet the average slave devised an alternative system for acquiring knowledge, even though learning to read and write seemed beyond the realm of reality. Plantation slaves generally were isolated from their masters and from the flow of ideas and information. The institution of slavery inhibited blacks from acquiring local and national information; but blacks, having come from a verbal society, developed the "slave grapevine," in which information—reports from the big house, local, national, and even international news—was widely and rapidly disseminated not only to the immediate plantation but to other plantations great distances away.[60]

Every plantation had a grapevine. Slaves listened carefully to their masters' conversations on politics or about other slaves. At the first opportunity, the reports were taken to the quarters, giving the slaves news of events and forewarning them of possible danger. Slaves were also conscious of events in the North, which were reported by slaves who had traveled with their masters or by free Negroes who could read. Since slaves were considered property—things—they were often invisible and had little or no difficulty overhearing their masters' conversations. Although always ready to play the role of the fool or ignoramus when necessary, slaves discussed such issues as the Fugitive Slave Law, abolitionism, Lincoln's campaign for president, and whether the Civil War would result in freedom for them.[61] Thus, under the most adverse conditions, and with no opportunities provided by the system to acquire knowledge, slaves, in their own fashion, obtained a degree of knowledge that would have astounded their owners, had they been privy to the inner sanctums of plantation life.

The tragedy of the slave's great desire for knowledge is reflected in the efforts of one Jamie Parker, who, knowing the consequences he faced if caught learning to read and write, was not deterred from his quest. As a young boy, Parker convinced a free Negro by the name of Scipio to teach him, in secret, the fundamentals. And Jamie, under rather poor circumstances, learned to spell and read limited parts from the Bible. Some months after his studies began, he was caught by the patrol. He was punished by the patrol and beaten on his naked back by his overseer, who himself could neither read nor write. The child's cuts were washed with salt water as added warning for this act of transgression. Scipio, for his part, was put to death. Yet, even this did not deter some from seeking and acquiring the magic powers locked in the written word. In fact mutilation—the cutting off of a thumb and forefinger— became a badge within the slave quarters, for it symbolized an attempted education. Further, education—the ability to read and write—provided the slave with immeasurable status in the slave quarters. Despite the legal restrictions and sanctions against it, slaves had invested education with mystical qualities and felt it was worth any amount of hardship.[62]

But the system did afford learning to slaves who performed certain tasks on the plantation—primarily the domestic servants and skilled artisans and craftsmen on plantations and in urban areas. On large plantations, economic efficiency dictated that certain slaves be taught particular skills and allowed to achieve a certain degree of knowledge in spite of the legal system and the alleged inferiority of blacks. Domestic servants comprised coachmen, laundresses, seamstresses, cooks, footmen, butlers, housemaids, chambermaids, children's nurses, and personal servants. Their day-to-day contact with the slaveholders enhanced their knowledge and sometimes led to their actually learning to read and write; slaves, in this latter instance, were taught either by benevolent masters or their young children. Lewis Clarke, a slave child, was one example of a slave having been taught to read and write by a white playmate. Clarke diligently spent his free time developing his new talents until he was caught by his mistress who, in an uproar, threatened him if he ever spelled another word.[63]

Another select and highly prized group of slaves produced by the peculiar institution were the craftsmen: engineers, coopers, carpenters blacksmiths, brickmakers, stonemasons, mechanics, shoemakers, weavers, millers, and landscapers. Even if many of these jobs did not require an actual ability to read and write, they did require a knowledge of figures. They also provided a measure of freedom which allowed the slaves time to cultivate their talents. Some turned out to be excellent craftsmen who produced outstanding work, so much so, that often their owners viewed them in a more favorable light than free artisans who worked on their plantations. It was ironic that after praising their intelligence and skill, the slaveholder could then turn and talk of the ignorance and utter hopelessness of the black race; it was a prime example of how the slave system required compartmentalization on the part of the slaveholders.[64] Sterling Spero and Abram Harris in their book, *The Black Worker*, discussed the skilled black laborer:

> . . . the ablest and most promising slaves who were not assigned to service in the great house were trained in the skilled crafts. The plantations were to a large extent self-sustaining units which did practically all their own repairing and made a large proportion of their own supplies. The masters found it easier and cheaper to have their slaves trained in carpentry, masonry, blacksmithing, and the other mechanical trades than to depend upon outside free white labor.[65]

The opportunity for black persons to gain a foothold in training for skilled occupations was, as during the colonial period, primarily determined by the exigencies of the plantation. The slave who had acquired the necessary training to be an artisan was of considerable value in contrast to the field hand. It was not unusual for a trained mechanic to sell for twice that of a very strong field hand. In some cases the plantation owners would hire out the labor of skilled slaves in the cities to either white master craftsmen or directly to the public. The slave artisan was important because he served as a privileged element among the slaves, and had a certain degree of freedom. Some planters permitted the skilled slave to hire out his own time, with the master getting a percentage of the money or the slave retaining a fixed income from his gross. Sometimes slaves hired out to contractors would do extra work and would keep this added income for themselves.[66]

While the specific features of plantation slavery generally inhibited the degree of skill a slave artisan on a plantation might have when compared with black mechanics in the cities, slave artisans were nonetheless a significant force in the development of black leadership. Many of the slave mechanics who hired out their labor could eventually buy their freedom and become actively engaged in either education or the abolitionist movement. Restrictive legislation designed to limit the number of free blacks meant some slaves accepted the protection and patronage of the white master even though they could have purchased their freedom. However, whenever it was possible, many black people sought total freedom for themselves and their families and set about the task of creating and developing a black community, i.e., black self-help institutions. A number of black leaders during the antebellum period were in fact trained as mechanics. Denmark Vesey, Nat Turner, Richard Allen, and Absolom Jones were outstanding representatives of this group.[67]

In spite of the interests of the planter class and its needs, black people sought to make progress beyond the boundaries prescribed by slavery and repressive racist legislation, but the magnificent effort by black people to overcome the barriers of institutionalized oppression caused a reaction among white skilled workers. Most efforts to legally curtail the opportunities of black skilled workers emanated from white skilled workers who feared that blacks would displace them in the job market. Thus blacks were faced with legal restrictions as well as mob violence and race riots in their efforts to earn a living.[68]

The use of contracted slave labor over white labor led, in some places, to a monopoly by black labor in certain occupations driving out white workers.[69] Black labor had an economic competitive edge over white labor because of its lower cost. It had political advantage inasmuch as it was backed by the power of the planter class. However, free black skilled workers or those skilled slaves free to hire out their labor were made the object of repressive legislation.

We have seen the extensive legislative restrictions placed on the education of blacks; some states went so far as to pass legislation to prohibit black slave labor from the building trades.[70] This reaction on the part of skilled white workers, and poor white farmers as well, was a response to the institution of slavery, which was in direct competition with more expensive forms of labor. But while this reaction was grounded in the political-economic basis of slavery, the subjective conception of white workers was that black people were to blame for their problems, which led to legal and physical attacks on black people. Indeed, this forced Frederick Douglass to remark:

> Prejudice against the free colored people in the United States has shown itself nowhere so invincible as among mechanics. The farmer and the professional man cherish no feeling so bitter as that cherished by these.

The latter would starve us out of the country entirely. At this moment I can more easily get my son in a lawyer's office to study law than I can into a blacksmith's shop to blow the bellows and wield the sledge hammer. Denied the means of learning useful trades we are pressed into the narrowest limits to obtain a livelihood.[71]

Douglass understood that the nature of working-class black-white hostility was rooted in slavery and in the role of the slavemaster, who pitted the two groups against each other. Yet despite the attempt to obstruct the growth of black skilled labor, blacks outnumbered whites in skilled trades in the South one hundred thousand to twenty thousand in 1865. While a few slaves were able to obtain skills, education was closed to the vast majority of slaves. As one southerner put it, "knowledge and slavery are incompatible."[72] Even those slaves who were skilled were not taught to read and write, let alone given the opportunity to think about pursuits beyond their function as artisans.

Education generally was at a very low level in the South, even for most whites. Statistics show that in 1840 only 5.72 percent of the white population in slaveholding states were pupils compared to 18.41 percent in non-slaveholding states. While slaveholding states had less than one-half of the white population of the northern states (some 6.1 million compared to 13.2 million), the South had less than a third as many schools, one-twentieth as many public libraries, and one-sixth as many books in libraries.[73]

The structure of the economy played a vital role in the South's policy toward education. Concentration on cotton production, lack of urbanization, and grossly unequal distribution of income were among the factors contributing to this situation. Also the planter class felt that public education, or any education which would require a high per capita expenditure, would result in funds being diverted from direct investment in production. This attitude was carried over into Reconstruction.[74]

Thus, slavery was an economic system designed to increase maximum productivity of the slaveholder's investment. The very nature of the system precluded provisions for slave education, since planters correctly understood that educating the slave population would result in the very destruction of the system they desired to perpetuate. In a very real sense, slavery was the worst barrier which prevented blacks from acquiring an education; but because the planter class needed certain functions performed, a limited number of slaves gained skills. The remainder had to depend upon their limited resources for knowledge. This thirst for knowledge was carried over into the Reconstruction period, but as will be seen in the next chapter, the economic interests of southerners coincided with those of northerners to inhibit black aspirations for education.

Free Blacks: Their Quest for Education

Most northern and southern whites believed that blacks were inferior. This alleged inferiority led them to the conclusion that blacks were incapable of learning; therefore, there was no need to provide schools for them. Free Negroes in the South were faced with the problem of securing their own education or doing without; most did without. Free blacks had a greater opportunity for education in urban centers. As early as 1810, free people of color in Charleston, South Carolina organized the Minor Society to provide an education for orphaned children.[75]

The vast majority of southern free blacks were denied an education because of their inability to secure funds to support a private school. Further, the activities of the abolitionists generated fear in southerners that their incendiary literature might adversely affect the free population. In conjunction with this, the various slave plots and insurrections, the most famous being the Vesey Plot and Turner Rebellion, caused fear to spread throughout the South. In an effort to end the threats and fears of slave rebellion, the little education available to free blacks was sharply curtailed. State after state passed laws that prohibited the distribution of abolitionist literature, that closed the schools and banned the instruction of free blacks, and in some instances passed laws that denied the free blacks movement in and out of the state. By the beginning of the Civil War, legal restrictions on free blacks were so severe that the acquisition of an education was nearly impossible.[76]

Legal restrictions of the northern states also severely hampered the educational development of northern free blacks. Northern attitudes were as much conditioned by racial prejudice as were southern attitudes. The idea of black and white children attending mixed schools was repugnant to most whites. Many northern states excluded free blacks from their schools altogether, while those that offered some schooling to blacks established separate facilities for them.[77]

As support for public education increased throughout the North, blacks found that they had to resort more and more to private education. Blacks, taxed as others, resented that they were unable to benefit from public schools. But even as states grudgingly assumed some responsibility for black education, they provided segregated facilities staffed by unqualified instructors. In

New York, for example, the Board of Education spent $1,600 for whites (buildings and sites) for every dollar spent for blacks, even though the black to white ratio was one to forty.[78]

Throughout the North, blacks fought against the imposition of segregated education facilities. They believed that segregation was a relic of slavery that fostered further prejudice and discrimination. Yet northern blacks succeeded in cracking legally imposed segregation only in Boston. In 1846, eighty-six blacks petitioned the Boston school committee to integrate the city's educational system, maintaining that the segregated Negro school was an insult. They failed to obtain results through their petitions, and Benjamin Roberts, on behalf of his daughter who had to pass five white schools to get to the black school, sued to force the city to integrate. Charles Summer, assisted by Robert Morris, who was black, carried the case to the State Supreme Court where the court upheld the school committee and first enunciated the separate–but–equal doctrine. Only after the state legislature prohibited segregated public education in April 1855, was the black school closed in Boston and the students integrated into the system.[79]

Carter G. Woodson listed a number of institutions founded for the education of blacks prior to 1861, among which were Avery College, Allegheny City, Pennsylvania (1849); and Wilberforce University, Xenia, Ohio (1856). White institutions of higher education permitted a few blacks to enter their halls of learning prior to 1861, the most noted of which was Oberlin College in Ohio. In fact, over 245 black students attended Oberlin before the war, comprising 3 percent of the total number. However, only a few of the students at Oberlin were in the college department, and of those that were, not all completed their undergraduate education.

There were only twenty-eight known black college graduates in the United States by the time of the Civil War, and not all of these had been educated in the United States. Four and one-half million blacks were severely handicapped with such a small number of black college graduates to serve as degreed leaders of their race. Even worse, there is recorded only one known black college teacher, Charles L. Reason, who taught at New York Central College at McGrawsville, New York.[81]

The law, coupled with race prejudice, severely hindered the efforts of free blacks to acquire an education prior to 1861. As pointed out later, whites generally were so hostile to black educational advancement that they even attempted, and often succeeded, in destroying the efforts of those who sought to facilitate black educational achievement. Blacks, both slave and free, could only hope that the approaching conflict between North and South would lead to a change in their legal status and thus enhance their opportunities for education and subsequent economic and political advancement.

Colonizationists, Abolitionists, and Education

The first quarter of the nineteenth century witnessed the rise of movements which had a primary impact on black education. The colonization movement was designed to remove free blacks from the United States, while the abolitionist movement was aimed at the elimination of the institution of slavery. Both movements had an impact on the education of black Americans, but for different reasons.

Following the revolutionary war, various groups of Americans opposed slavery, but were unsure of the best method for solving the problem. Some thought that the best way was the removal—forced or voluntary—of Negroes from the United States to such diverse places as Canada, the Caribbean, Central and South America, and of course to their ancestral homeland, Africa. Thomas Jefferson, who wrote "all men are created equal," was torn between the evil of slavery and his belief that blacks and whites could not reside together in this country. His belief stemmed from the alleged inferiority of blacks. One means of ridding the nation of slavery and solving the problem of black citizenship was the removal of blacks through colonization. Jefferson basically embodied early anti-slavery thought: freedom for the slaves was one thing; living with them another.[82]

Many people discussed the merits of colonization, but Paul Cuffe, a black sea captain, was the first to take positive action. Cuffe, the son of an American Indian mother and black father, transported thirty-eight free Negroes to West Africa. Cuffe believed that Africans should be "civilized" through a transfusion of American Negroes into the continent. After the first voyage, he realized that his venture was too expensive to support privately, therefore government funds were necessary to continue the endeavor.[83]

Except for a few isolated ventures, the central movement was organized and sustained by whites. In December 1816, in the House of Representatives' chamber in Washington, The American Society for Colonizing the Free People of Color in the United States was formed. The scheme was initiated by the Reverend Robert Finley. The American Colonization Society, as it was popularly called, was headed by Justice Bushrod Washington, nephew of the first president of the United States, and backed by such leading American figures as James Madison, James Monroe, Andrew Jackson, and Henry Clay.

In 1819 Congress gave $100,000, ostensibly to establish a government agency in Africa, to resettle victims of the African slave trade. The following year, the society "purchased" Cape Mesurado for $300 and named the acquisition Liberia, with Monrovia, after President James Monroe, as its capital. This private colony, an anomaly on the West African coast, was granted its independence in 1847. At a cost of $2.5 million, the society settled only 12,000 immigrants.[84]

The American Colonization Society left a negative impression on most blacks. Reverend Finley, because he was appalled at the misery and ignorance of the free black population in the North, considered the society a benevolent organization. Finley thought that blacks were capable of improving their condition, but not in the United States. He felt that God had intended Africans to remain in Africa. The society labored hard to convince blacks that it was in their best interest to leave the United States where they could never achieve dignity and equality. But blacks overwhelmingly rejected this idea.[85]

The American Colonization Society had a wide variety of interest groups within its program: free blacks, missionaries, empire builders, trading interest groups, northern liberal whites, and southern whites. It is interesting to note that the few free blacks who joined the movement desired to escape the oppression of American society, while at the other political extreme southern slaveholders desired to remove the free black population from their midst, since they were viewed as a threat to the system of slavery.[86]

In spite of the oppression and injustice, blacks were determined to remain. At a Fourth of July celebration, Peter Williams, pastor of St. Phillips Episcopal Church in New York, expressed the views of a majority of free blacks:

> Though delivered from the fetters of slavery, we are oppressed by an unreasonable, unrighteous, and cruel prejudice, which aims at nothing less than the forcing away of all the free colored people of the United States to the distant shores of Africa.
>
> We are NATIVES of this country, we ask to be treated as well as FOREIGNERS. Not a few of our fathers suffered and bled to purchase its independence; we ask only to be treated as well as those who fought against it. We have toiled to cultivate it, and to raise it to its present prosperous condition; we ask only to share equal privileges with those who come from distant lands, to enjoy the fruits of our labour.
>
> It is very certain that very few free people of colour *wish* to go to

land. The colonization Society *knows* this, and yet they do certainly calculate that in time they will have us all removed there.

How can this be effected by making our situation worse here, and closing every other door against us?[87]

In evaluating the impact of the colonizationists on black education, one could easily conclude that they served as what might be described as negative facilitators. First, the more liberal members provided free blacks opportunities for higher education with the hope that they would eventually become so discontent with their situation in this country that they would migrate to Liberia. Others, including most southern colonizationists, accepted the idea of educating blacks provided they left the country. Those who remained should be kept in ignorance for fear that education would lead to either their freedom or their extermination.[88]

Although colonizationists were willing to educate blacks, the provision requiring emigration had an overall negative influence on the race. The colonizationists began early to develop the intellectual growth of blacks in their efforts to prepare them to hold responsible positions in Liberia and Haiti. They were taught mechanical arts, agriculture, science, and biblical literature. Those with exceptional abilities were given special training as teachers, preachers, and physicians. Higher educational institutions were actually started to promote the colonizationist cause; one in 1817 at Parsippany, New Jersey, offered a four-year course.[89]

Thus, some of the best organized efforts for Negro higher education provided opportunities only to those willing to leave the country. If the scheme had worked, the process would have effectively drained the free black population of its most talented members, but the scheme failed because of the strong and consistent opposition of free Negroes and white abolitionists.[90] Blacks unyieldingly opposed colonization because it was strictly an attempt by whites to rid the nation of free blacks. The abolitionists not only opposed the efforts of the colonizationists, but did much to facilitate education among the free black population.

The abolitionist movement had two distinct periods: what could be called the pre-Garrison (before 1830) and Garrisonian (after 1830) eras. The pro-slavery argument hinged on the inferiority of blacks and, in many instances, the pre-Garrison abolitionists accepted this view. Prior to 1830, their efforts consisted primarily of persuasion and conciliation. The abolitionists were quiet-mannered men, usually of property and good standing in their communities, and often were laymen in the church. They sought a gradual rather than immediate abolition of slavery. Many believed that colonization—deportation to Africa—might just be the best long-range solution.[91]

By the 1830s slavery was not dying out, but was flourishing. Cotton was king and spreading westward. In spite of abolitionist activities, the South was ready to contest the North for control of the West. These events coincided with the rise in the Garrisonian era of a new breed of abolitionists, who favored more direct action. Militant abolitionists, led by William Lloyd Garrison, reflected the revolutionism of Nat Turner and the strength of David Walker. They demanded the immediate abolition of slavery as well as improvement in the political and economic position of northern Negroes. Many of the new leaders felt that one could not separate slaves from free Negroes since both shared the same plight. Unlike the colonizationists, abolitionists came to believe that blacks should be educated to live as free men in the United States. They believed further that if blacks were educated, prejudice would be abated and the need to expatriate them would likewise be reduced.[92]

A major flaw in the abolitionist movement stemmed from many participants' inability to accept social intercourse with blacks. Many abolitionists had not escaped the overwhelming prejudice of the society at large. Since most Americans believed that blacks were inferior, race mixing was extremely unpopular. This created dissension within the movement; one example of this took place in the Female Anti-Slavery Society in Fall River, Massachusetts. The society was nearly dissolved over the invitation extended to several colored women to join. The opposition stemmed not from black women's attendance, but from the idea that their membership would place them as equals with white women. After much debate, they were finally admitted.[93]

Abolitionists often accepted the popular stereotypes of blacks and even perpetuated them in their newspapers and abolitionist literature. Some went so far as to express concern when Frederick Douglass, because of his rapid intellectual development, no longer fitted the stereotype of a slave. Yet, abolitionists made some notable successes by 1860, in the face of powerful public hostility and racial prejudice. Much of the success of the abolitionists can be attributed to the ability of blacks to criticize abolitionists as well as to the determination of those whites who believed that their devotion to the cause of blacks necessitated integration of the races.[94]

The abolitionists did more than any group to facilitate the education of blacks prior to 1861. Most northern states either excluded blacks altogether or provided separate education for them. Education was the foremost aspiration of northern Negroes; with it they hoped to improve their status. The threat of interracial education aroused more prejudice and hatred than anything else in the North, because most viewed this arrangement as tantamount to racial amalgamation; thus, white abolitionists found themselves in a hostile environment.[95]

The early abolitionists showed considerable interest in Negro education. The New York Society's pride was the African Free School, which remained independent for forty-seven years until it came under city support in 1834. In March of the following year, twenty-eight whites and fourteen blacks attended integrated classes at the newly established Noyes Academy in Canaan, New Hampshire. The board, which included several abolitionists, set out a policy which admitted all qualified candidates regardless of race. Abolitionists enthusiastically endorsed the academy, but the experiment was short-lived when townspeople destroyed the school in August 1835.[96]

Institutions of higher education were slow to open their doors to blacks. The first known black college graduate was Alexander Lucius Twilight, who received his B.A. degree in August 1823 from Middlebury College in Vermont. Edward Jones, the second black graduate, entered Amherst College in 1822 (the second year of the college's existence) and finished August 1826. Amherst did not graduate another black until after the Civil War. In fact, prior to 1840 there is no record to indicate that more than fifteen blacks entered white colleges. Free blacks and white abolitionists concluded that what was needed were separate Negro colleges.[97]

Free blacks and abolitionists desired to establish institutions in which labor would be combined with academics to enable the poorest students to acquire an education. In the District of Columbia, Miss Myrtilla Minor spearheaded the movement when she established a school for girls. Opposition soon developed to providing an education for blacks which was "far above their social and political condition." The girls and teachers were insulted and abused. Finally, in 1860, because of lack of police protection, the school was set afire.[98]

In spite of these setbacks, there were some successful endeavors. Ashmun Institute, now Lincoln University, was established in Pennsylvania, and incorporated under Presbyterian auspices in 1854. The first higher educational institution to be controlled by blacks was Wilberforce University near Xenia, Ohio. The school was first under the control of the Methodist Episcopal Church, and then the African Methodist Episcopal Church secured the transfer of the property through the efforts of the Rev. Daniel A. Payne and his associates.[99]

During the 1850s, the Fugitive Slave Act created a great amount of hostility within the abolitionist community. The Kansas-Nebraska Act opened slavery in an area where it had been banned since 1820. The *Dred Scott* decision was further cause for demoralization. More militant abolitionists reacted: John Brown seized the government arsenal at Harpers Ferry, October 1859. The following year Abraham Lincoln was elected president. Soon thereafter South Carolina seceded from the Union and America was in the midst of a Civil War.[100] Abolitionists, and in a negative way, colonizationists, had done much to encourage black education, but not nearly enough to offset slavery in the South and racial prejudice and discrimination in the North.

By the beginning of the Civil War, the American system of enslavement, with its concomitant system of race prejudice and discrimination, had effectively denied blacks the opportunity for an education. Part of the justification for the enslavement of African people was based on their alleged inferiority and inability to learn. This contorted logic formed the philosophical basis for subsequent inequitable relationships with black people and led to the establishment of a legal system that was designed to repress blacks, both slave and free. The peculiar institution became economically entrenched in the southern way of life, and was reinforced by a highly developed legal and philosophical system. Free blacks were a threat to the slave system as well as an assumed threat to the white working class of the North. The only organized effort to provide some measure of education to black people came through the work of two groups, one of which wanted to provide blacks with an education as a means to make them self-sufficient once they were deported. Yet, in spite of these disadvantages, blacks struggled to acquire knowledge in the hope of improving their plight.

The oppressive nature of the system was so overwhelming that at the time of the Civil War only a miniscule number out of the 4.5 million blacks could read and write. Southern civilization was built on the sweat and toil of black people. In the North, blacks were forced into menial jobs which whites would no longer accept. Following the war, the nation played a cruel trick on black people who remained in the middle of the continuing sectional struggle for economic and political ascendance. Overnight blacks were estranged as their former masters turned their backs on them. The nation as a whole made a half-hearted attempt to rectify generations of injustices, but the attempt was short-lived.

BLACK PEOPLE DURING THE POST-CIVIL WAR PERIOD, 1865-1890

THE CIVIL WAR AND ITS AFTERMATH

The era from the end of the Civil War to the end of the nineteenth century is extremely important in the history of Afro-Americans in this country. A recapitulation of the major events relating to blacks and an analysis of those events illuminate the subsequent plight of black people in America and attest to why affirmative action programs are justified.

The post-Civil War era was the time in which white Americans were trying to decide what place the former slaves would have in American society. The beginning looked hopeful. The Freedmen's Bureau was formed and provided great assistance to blacks in their effort to help themselves. This was the first, and until recently the only, major effort on the part of the federal government, to help blacks overcome the injustices of the slave system. To overcome the prejudice and discrimination of the postwar era, the federal government passed various Reconstruction amendments and civil rights acts. But eventually these acts were impeded by the racial attitudes prevalent throughout the country, the economic interests of capitalists, and finally the law itself, which was used to repress blacks.

Although this narrative ends just prior to the beginning of the twentieth century, when it was evident that the national intent was to relegate black people to a position slightly above their previous condition of servitude, the picture is not totally negative. Throughout the period, blacks themselves made tremendous efforts to acquire an education in the face of extreme opposition. This enduring faith in education as a panacea was a carryover from the slavery period. With the advent of emancipation, the magic of the written word was surrounded with an even greater aura. The newly emancipated blacks, like most of their contemporaries, believed that education was the key to the future.

The reasons why the Civil War was fought depend in large measure on who is doing the explaining and at what particular time in history the explanation is given. Slavery has been viewed by some as the central issue which precipitated the war, while others have viewed slavery as a peripheral issue. Although the war was fought for a variety of reasons, it is clear that slavery as an economically viable institution desperately needed to expand westward for survival. It is equally true that northerners, regardless of how they felt about black people, were opposed to the expansion of slavery into territories that directly interfered with the free labor market, that depressed the value of free labor, and that demoralized the white workmen who had to compete with slave labor.[1]

It does not seem unfair to say that even during the Civil War, the views of whites in the North and South were not that divergent. Economic questions and racial attitudes were intertwined just as they had been during the slavery period. The South needed to expand slavery not only for its economic existence but also for its social and political survival. The northern position on slavery was complex, but as early as 1861 a majority of northern whites were not in favor of emancipation of the slaves. In fact, when in July 13, 1863, the Union began the process to raise three hundred thousand men through the draft in New York City, one of the most disastrous and diabolical riots occurred in which whites vented their hatred on defenseless and innocent blacks, as well as on abolitionists and other Union sympathizers. The riots indicated the extent to which northerners opposed the war and, especially, Negro emancipation.[2]

As the end of the Civil War approached, the question of slavery and the place black Americans were to assume in society was not resolved. The whole question of race had become embroiled inexplicably in the question of economic self-interest. The southern economic system rested on slavery; at the same time both free and enslaved black people were perceived by northerners as a cheap labor force that would undercut the earning power of white labor. Slavery had served well the economic interest of capitalists in both the

North and South, but now it threatened to destroy the nation and had to be curtailed.

Lincoln, prior to his election as president, felt that slavery must be stopped where it was, and ultimately eliminated. He thought it was impossible for the country to be half-slave and half-free and remain a nation. Although Lincoln was disturbed by the way blacks were mistreated in slavery, he did not believe in racial equality. Because slaves were viewed as property protected by the Constitution, few politicians were willing to interfere with slavery without compensation. When Congress passed, and Lincoln approved on April 16, 1862, a bill freeing the slaves in the District of Columbia, the bill allowed payment of up to $300 for each emancipated slave. Lincoln, in part, issued his preliminary Emancipation Proclamation September 22, 1862, for fear that if he failed to act, England would recognize the confederacy. The final version of the Emancipation Proclamation was issued on January 1, 1863, but it freed only those slaves in states or parts thereof in rebellion against the United States.[3] Thus it was not until the adoption of the Thirteenth Amendment, December 18, 1865, that all 4 million blacks were freed from bondage.

Events which took place following the Civil War were contingent upon how people viewed the new freedmen and how they perceived the economic role blacks would play in the new order. The years from 1865 to 1890 are a history of America's attempts to find an acceptable place for blacks. Although black people determined their own destiny to an extent, it is also clear that negative attitudes towards blacks created hostile reactions and therefore negative results. The one positive affirmative action, the creation of the Freedmen's Bureau, resulted from positive attitudes by some Congressmen; but the overall effort, which was not long lasting, was quantitatively and qualitatively insufficient.

Lincoln's plan for Reconstruction allowed white southerners more or less free rein in their efforts to reconstruct the South. Southerners' actions after the war indicated that the years of bloody warfare had not changed their attitudes; in fact they proceeded to act as though the old order would soon return, with the exception that slaves would be free. What happened after Appomattox is very much related to the protracted southern attitudes toward blacks, as well as the economic crisis which occurred after the war. Since South Carolina suffered considerable damage and was among the first states to enact the black codes, it is worth examining in detail.

Sherman left a trail of desolation as he worked through South Carolina, leaving it in ruin in many places. The leading city of Charleston had not overcome the destruction caused by the fire of 1861. What railroads were not destroyed were eventually worn out during the war. The state bank was obligated to suspend its operations. Many other banks were ruined by loans made to the confederate government. Land was confiscated from planters who failed to pay their taxes and sold at a reduction of its original value; farm production, as a result, decreased. To add to the confusion, the crime rate was rising in some remote districts, but probably the greatest loss to the state was the loss of human life. Not many families were able to escape without the mourning of a loved one. The South generally suffered more loss of life in relation to the total white population than did the North.[4]

Coupled with the general economic problems of the states was the problem—or what was perceived as a problem by the whites—of the freedmen. The 1860 Census revealed that South Carolina had a white population of 291,388 and a black population of 402,406 slaves and 9,914 free people of color. The blacks were determined to test their new-found freedom. This was accomplished in a number of ways, but of most concern to whites was the desire of freedmen to leave the plantation. Whites also highly resented what they believed was the insubordination of blacks.[5]

What was true in South Carolina was generally true throughout the South. Four million blacks in the South gained their freedom with scarcely more than the clothes on their backs. The southern economy was wrecked. With the social, economic, and political control of the blacks gone with the institution of slavery, whites felt that their entire social order had collapsed. Yet, as in the days of slavery, whites continued to believe that black people were inferior, and without some sort of social force or coercion, would return to their barbarous state and carry what remained of southern civilization with them. A new method had to be devised to control blacks. Southern whites resorted to what became known as the Black Codes. When the codes were overturned by radicals in Congress, southerners used extralegal means to accomplish their ends. The codes had an extremely significant negative impact on the education of black people in the South. Although there is no mention of education in the various acts passed under the codes, it was assumed that blacks could not benefit from education. This attitude was a carry-over from slavery and continued to exist into the twentieth century.

The first states to pass Black Codes were South Carolina and Mississippi, and other states followed the pattern. Although other states might not have passed such stringent measures, the codes from South Carolina and Mississippi were those first seen by Congress. The Radicals concluded that the South had not repented and had desired to reenslave the freedmen.[6]

South Carolina began the process of reconstructing itself when delegates met in convention, September 13, 1865, to revise the Constitution. The convention repealed the ordinance of secession, abolished slavery, and recognized that the United States government had emancipated the slaves. The question of the freedmen's rights came up only in relation to the general agreement that South Carolina's restructured Constitution and government were for whites only. Before the convention adjourned, it instructed the governor to appoint a commission to draw up a code to regulate the freedmen. The commission was to report to the legislature and the legislature was to alter the laws of the state accordingly.[7]

The code was entitled "A Bill to establish and regulate the Domestic Relations of Persons of Color, and to amend the law in relation to Paupers, Vagrance, and Bastardy."[8] The code began with a definition of Negro as a person with one-eighth or more Negro blood, and all persons so defined were subject to the provisions of the code. They were given the right to acquire and dispose of property, sue and be sued, make contracts, receive the fruits of their labor, and receive the protection of their persons and property under the law unless so modified. Persons of color received the right of trial and the right to testify in court if they were considered competent witnesses. Generally, the laws regulating property and the disposal thereof were identical for whites and blacks. Marriages between blacks before and after their emancipation were declared legal, removing the stigma of illegitimacy from the children.

Other laws were formulated strictly for Negroes. The death penalty was prescribed for persons of color convicted of homicide, assaulting a white person, and seeking to have intercourse with a white woman. The code stated that servants who assaulted their master, employer, or his family would be whipped. Written permission was required before "servants" could sell the products from masters' farms. Persons of color were forbidden from serving in the militia, and bearing firearms unless they had written permission from a district judge. Only farmers were permitted to own shotguns for hunting purposes. To manufacture liquor for, or to sell liquor to, Negroes was strictly forbidden. Negroes from outside the state were not permitted to enter unless bonded. Marriages between whites and Negroes were declared illegal and void.

An elaborate system of contract labor was developed. "All persons who should make contracts for service or labor should be known as servants, and those with whom they should contract should be known as masters." The relationship between master and servants was described in detail. Hours for servants—farm or domestic—were prescribed by the code. Precautions were taken to prevent the overworking of servants by masters, and what was considered reasonable work assignments were listed. Indolence by servants was forbidden. A time limitation was set for servants who wished to visit or to receive visitors. A clause was inserted which gave servants the right to leave their employment under certain conditions, and in some cases, to recover any wages due them. Blacks were restricted to a limited type of employment, mainly manual labor and domestic service.

Provisions were included for the care of paupers, and punishment was provided for vagrants. A series of district courts was set up to ensure that the provisions of the code were justly administered.

At a special session of the legislature, which met Tuesday, September 4, 1866, the code was slightly modified to accommodate the objections of the military authorities to the color provisions of the court section, but the basic code was left intact.

The modified code strikingly resembled the antebellum slave code for no other reason than the legislature's belief that there existed a need to prescribe and regulate the conduct of the freedmen. But there were more similarities. The freedmen were not granted state citizenship. Any right or privilege held had to be specified, and those not granted were expressly denied. Of course, with the abolition of slavery, the right of absolute control over blacks was lost. Protective provisions, such as a limit on the number of hours a laborer could be worked, were often retained. Punishments for insubordination and assault upon whites were as harsh as punishments under the slave code. During the antebellum period, the free persons of color continuously had to prove themselves free, and in contrast to the difficulties of antebellum free blacks, the freedman had to prove he was not a vagrant; the freedman had to have permission to be where he was at all times.[9]

Thus, the Black Codes were the embodiment of white attitudes toward the freedmen. Just as whites believed that blacks were shiftless and, unless forced to work, unproductive, whites also believed that blacks were so inferior that educating them was a waste of time and money.[10] It is quite evident that the codes were negative barriers to Negro education. The South not only failed to provide some sort of education for the freedmen but also instituted codes that were designed to assure a steady, cheap supply of labor. The southerners felt that education would only make blacks indolent and discontent.

Southerners also resented that others were desirous of assisting the former slaves, the vast majority of whom were illiterate. White people in

Virginia were shocked to see northern whites educating blacks. Two teachers, who went by boat to Fayette, North Carolina, to establish a school for blacks, were refused landing privileges by the sheriff. The presence of federal troops was needed to protect teachers in South Carolina's black schools from native whites, who had grown intolerant of the teachers' presence.[11]

Violence against blacks and Union sympathizers became systematic with the rise of the Ku Klux Klan. Much of this violence was aimed at blacks who wished to acquire an education. The Klan originated in Pulaski, Tennessee, in the law office of Judge Thomas M. Jones in the spring of 1866. From this beginning, the Klan spread throughout the South. In North Carolina, for example, the Klan embraced three orders: The White Brotherhood, The Constitutional Union Guard, and the Invisible Empire.[12]

The Klan was also responsible for numerous violent attacks on white teachers and their black students in the South (most of which went unpunished). On July 4, 1868, the Klan in Bedford County, Tennessee, whipped two men: a black and a white northerner, both of whom taught at the Negro school. The teachers received two hundred lashes after having suffered a variety of indignities. The same year in St. Helena Parish, Louisiana, the Klan burned two Negro churches, a schoolhouse, and killed several blacks before the night ended.[13]

Klan activity was not limited to discouraging those who were interested in providing elementary education for blacks. Berea College in Kentucky had been founded for both blacks and whites in 1855 by abolitionists from Oberlin College in Ohio. The founders had to brave the resentment and open hostility of the local inhabitants. In 1871, the Klan was exceedingly active, and during the many outrages which took place, a trustee of Berea College was whipped by the local whites for associating with blacks. The college continued as an integrated institute until Kentucky passed a law which forced the school to segregate.[14]

From these and hundreds of other examples of beatings, lynchings, and burnings, by Klan organizations throughout the South, it was perfectly clear that what white southerners could not accomplish "legally" through the Black Codes was accomplished through extralegal means. Mob violence had a severely negative impact on black education, but it failed to stop blacks from attempting to acquire an education, and for the most part, failed to deter the dedicated whites who came south to teach the newly freed slaves. The Black Codes and mob violence influenced Congress to pass amendments to the Constitution and Civil Rights Acts which, for a while, gave blacks added protection and aided them in their efforts to acquire an education.

RECONSTRUCTION: PRESIDENT VS. CONGRESS

Reconstruction Under the Executive

While whites in the states proceeded to reconstruct the South in line with their traditional prejudices against black people, disputes of a larger nature and of greater significance loomed in the nation's capital. The argument over the nature of the recent conflict between the North and the South was now forming the basis for the debate between Congress and the President over the best methods of reconstructing the South. Both Congress and the President claimed authority to initiate and to execute Reconstruction. What position one held depended upon whether one believed that the southern states actually seceded from the Union.[15]

Numerous theories were developed. Basically, they can be reduced to two: 1) the presidential theory and 2) the congressional theory. Lincoln initiated, and Johnson retained, the theory that the southern states did not secede from the Union. These states were in rebellion; but after the rebellion had been crushed, the states' position under the Constitution had not been impaired. The congressional theorists maintained a difference of opinion on the principles involved and what policy demanded. The Radicals in Congress believed that the southern states had seceded and had forfeited all rights under the Constitution. They were now entirely dependent upon the federal government for pardon and restoration. Both the executive and legislative branches of government believed it their duty to reconstruct the South according to their political doctrine.[16]

Reconstruction was initiated in the Executive Department under Abraham Lincoln, who began presidential Reconstruction as early as January 11, 1864 in Louisiana. He thought it important to begin Reconstruction as soon as possible and to develop policies geared to the particular needs of individual states.[17] At the beginning of his second administration, Lincoln set forth the basic tenor of his policy in his inaugural address: "With malice toward none, with charity for all, with firmness in the right, as God gives us to see the right, let us finish the work we are in, to bind up the nation's wounds, to care for him who shall have borne the battle, and for his widow and his orphans, to do all which may achieve and cherish a just and a lasting peace among ourselves and with all nations."[18]

Upon Lincoln's death, April 15, 1865, Andrew Johnson, soon after taking office, adopted the main features of Lincoln's policy. In May 1865, Johnson issued a proclamation which pardoned all persons who had engaged in rebellion, except those persons who held high offices in the confederacy and confederate supporters who had more than $20,000 in property. Those persons who accepted the pardon were required to take an oath of loyalty to the national government. Johnson's plans were mainly political. Each state was required to elect members to a constitutional convention, adopt a new constitution in line with national developments, ratify the Thirteenth Amendment, and elect new members to local, state, and national offices. The franchise for the freedmen, their protection, and other provisions regarding the emancipated slaves were to be left to the individual states.[19]

From the actions of South Carolina, Mississippi, and other states, it was evident what the conservative South proposed for the freedmen. Blacks did better under the active backings of the "radicals" in Congress who proposed legislation that was initially intended to extend a measure of protection to the newly freed slaves.

Radical Reconstruction

The first task before Congress was to free all of the slaves, since Lincoln's Emancipation Proclamation fell short of the job. Many people assumed that the Thirteenth Amendment to the Constitution would automatically pass, especially after the 1864 elections and after the new Congress met in 1865, but it did not happen. Many Democrats had a distaste for emancipation. There was a lingering hatred for abolitionists, a belief that Lincoln had unnecessarily prolonged the war and that the war was to the benefit of the slaves, and, of course, there was general race prejudice. One congressman expressed the fear that the Thirteenth Amendment would not put to rest the question of slavery, since the nation would still be faced with the dispensation of the ex-slaves. The more astute congressmen recognized the need for additional constitutional and legislative protection.[20]

During the debates, the Democrats accused the Republicans of wanting to control the future of the United States government through the use of the Negro. The Republicans maintained that the opposite was true: the Democrats wanted to unite with the South to control national affairs. With the absence of some Democrats and the affirmative vote of others, the Amendment finally passed one hundred nineteen to fifty-six and was sent to the states for ratification.[21]

The passage of the amendment did not by any means usher in Radical Reconstruction. In fact, Andrew Johnson had emerged as the leader of the conservatives, who were expected to remain in power over the next fifty to one hundred years. Being a Democrat on a Republican ticket, Johnson was expected to receive the support of both parties, with the exception of the Chase-Sumner faction. But Johnson defeated himself and made the "radical" proposals appear for what they were—moderate. Johnson felt that whites were superior. His opposition to slavery was based upon his hatred of southern aristocratic rule. He was glad to see slavery end since its destruction effectively broke the rule of the planter class, but he believed that the protection of the freedman belonged to the states, and thus his policies were based on a minimum of interference in state affairs.[22]

Although the Republicans were not united on the question of Negro suffrage, most felt that blacks should have all other rights and privileges of freemen. Therefore, when Johnson vetoed the Freedmen's Bureau Bill in February, 1866, and the Civil Rights Act of March, his actions were viewed as a declaration of war. The extension of the life of the bureau had the support of Republicans in and outside of Congress. But southerners had clearly expressed their opposition to the bill, and Democrats felt that any action on behalf of the freedmen should be left to the various states and local governments. The Republicans in Congress, by no means radical, embraced the Stevens-Sumner plan of suffrage, confiscation of former confederate property, and prolonged territorial status for the South. Since neither bill included these provisions, the majority of congressmen were incensed at Johnson's actions in light of the Black Codes and other indications that the rights of freedmen needed protection. Congress overrode Johnson's veto and then united over the issue of freedmen's rights, where there was little agreement before.[23]

The Civil Rights Act itself provided that all persons born in the United States and not subject to foreign powers were citizens of the United States. Congress provided that all such citizens should enjoy the right of equality before the law in all states and territories. The federal courts were given exclusive jurisdiction over all cases where the rights secured by the act were denied or not enforced in state courts.[24]

Fearful that the Supreme Court would declare the act unconstitutional, Congress passed the Fourteenth Amendment and sent it to the states for ratification. Since approval of the amendment was a precondition for the reinstatement of southern states into the Union, and since three northern states rescinded its ratification, some questioned the legality of the amendment. Nevertheless, on July 28, 1868, the Fourteenth Amendment was declared part of the Constitution.[25]   The important sections of the amendment provided for:

All persons born or naturalized in the United States, and subject to the jurisdiction thereof, are citizens of the State wherein they reside. No State shall make or enforce any law which shall abridge the privileges and immunities of citizens of the United States; nor shall any state deprive any person of life, liberty or property, without due process of law; nor deny to any person within its jurisdiction the equal protection of the laws.[26]

An important, but never used, section of the amendment stated that when states denied its citizens—meaning blacks—the right to vote, their representation in Congress would be reduced accordingly. Congress gave itself power to enforce the provisions of the act with appropriate legislation.[27]

Following the adoption of the Fourteenth Amendment, Congress passed the Fifteenth Amendment and submitted it to the states for adoption. The amendment simply read:

The right of citizens of the United States to vote shall not be denied or abridged by the United States or by any State on account of race, color, or previous condition of servitude.

The Congress shall have power to enforce this article by appropriate legislation.[28]

With passage of the amendment, protests arose that the Republican party was trying to use the Negro vote to perpetuate itself. The few southern states still out of the Union had to ratify the amendment as a precondition for readmittance. New York rescinded her adoption, while California, Delaware, Kentucky, Maryland, Oregon, and Tennessee rejected it outright. Nevertheless, it was officially ratified March 30, 1870.[29]

Within five years after the ratification of the Fifteenth Amendment, Congress passed three important civil rights acts to implement the provisions of the Reconstruction amendments and to protect blacks from the violent outrages of the Ku Klux Klan, other terrorist organizations, and individuals. Under the first Enforcement Act, as they were called, of May 31, 1870, Congress imposed criminal sanctions for interference with the right of Negro suffrages as granted by the Fifteenth Amendment. The second act, passed February 28, 1871, provided for the appointment of election supervisors by federal courts and made interference with their duties a federal offense. This act was followed by the so-called Ku Klux Klan Act of April 20, 1871, which imposed penalties upon those persons who deprived any person or group of persons of those rights guaranteed by the Fourteenth Amendment.[30]

The federal government made one last attempt to secure the rights of blacks before Reconstruction officially ended in 1877. The Civil Rights Act of March 1, 1875, provided that all persons within the United States should have the right of access to places of public accommodation without regard to race, color, or previous condition of servitude. The act enabled the aggrieved party to recover up to $500 in damage; the federal courts were given exclusive jurisdiction in cases arising under the act. The act originally covered churches, but, according to one author, Senators ". . . evidently thought that such a prohibition laid too great a strain on institutions committed to brotherhood of man and struck out that provision." The Senate version also had banned segregated schools, but the ban was rejected by the House.[31]

This overview of Radical Reconstruction provides in capsule form the federal government's effort to extend and protect the rights of blacks. The effort was short-lived and totally inadequate for the task. Economic pressure and race prejudice were too strong to overcome the halfhearted effort to provide equality for blacks. Before discussing the end of Reconstruction, it is worthwhile to examine the work of the Freedmen's Bureau; the first real affirmative attempt on the part of the national government to compensate blacks for the injustices of slavery. The bureau, which did not remain in existence long enough and lacked the necessary financial support to assure its success, ultimately failed. But the bureau encouraged blacks to acquire an education and raise their status accordingly, and it provided some basis for the education of blacks where none had existed before.

The Freedmen's Bureau

One of the most positive, however limited, contributions made by the federal government was the establishment of the Bureau of Refugees, Freedmen, and Abandoned Lands, popularly called the Freedmen's Bureau. (The bureau also helped many whites.) The bureau was established March 3, 1865, and was headed by General O. O. Howard as a branch of the War Department. Its activities included the distribution of food, clothing, and other supplies, and provisions for job placement, homestead land, and educational facilities. Over President Johnson's veto, the life of the bureau was extended to July 16, 1866. The bureau's activities represented, for the first time, an extraordinary extension of direct federal aid to individuals.[32]

In spite of the bureau's many faults and problems, it did much to aid efforts of blacks to achieve an education. Some of its educational activities are worth recounting here. From 1865 to 1870, the bureau and interested northerners helped the freedmen to achieve the education they had long desired. With little money for the first year of operation, the bureau authorized the use of many federal buildings for rent-free schoolhouses. The bureau also provided transportation for teachers, distributed books, and helped private groups obtain government rations for their instructors at cost. But during the first year of the bureau's operation, its greatest educational achievement was the psychological support it provided many benevolent associations; it enthusiastically coordinated and supported the associations' work at a time when many were overpowered by the task at hand.[33]

After July 1866, the bureau provided more financial assistance. Congress gave the bureau $500,000 for rent and repairs of schools and asylums. The money the agency received from the sales of confederate property was used for a variety of educational purposes. Limited to the repair of buildings, the bureau required the freedmen to do all they could before the agency came to their rescue and completed the job.[34]

In Burke County, North Carolina, blacks had organized as early as 1867 in their attempt to establish schools for themselves. With the assistance of a white pastor, a committee was formed to raise money to purchase a lot on which to construct a school. Burke County blacks quickly raised $150 as a down payment on the lot. The bureau authorized money for the construction of the school. This was just one example of the more than six hundred thirty schoolhouses the bureau had built or helped build by March 1869 at a cost of $1,771,132. Over the next three years, appropriations came to $2 million.[35]

Twice a year the bureau made reports of its activities in the southern states. In July 1868, the bureau reported that North Carolina seemed to have made more progress in education than any other state. There was opposition to the bureau's efforts and the efforts of northerners. There was extreme hostility against a white woman who came to Wilmington to organize a school for poor whites. The general population and press opposed her school because she was a white woman from Boston, but through determination, the school succeeded.[36]

In the seventh report, the bureau indicated that when funds were available, schools continued into the summer months because people were so eager to learn. The fall term (1868) began late in a number of places because of crop harvesting. Opposition was widespread but subsided after the elections. The bureau was still faced with the same old prejudice and resistance to black equal rights which resulted in too little practical encouragement of Negro education. Nevertheless, the bureau could make the following report for selected states:

	Schools Supported Entirely by Freedmen	Schools Supported In Part by Freedmen	Buildings Furnished by the Bureau
Virginia	74	152	114
North Carolina	80	151	116
Georgia	18	88	18
Alabama	4	25	29
Texas	31	26	17

The following year, Congress severely curtailed the bureau's activities. Fortunately for blacks, the education department was one of several left in the South.[37]

Dr. H. C. Vogell, North Carolina Superintendent of Education, said of the freedmen's desire for an education: "Old men and women with spectacles, have come night after night, after their hard day's work was over, in order that they might be able to read the Bible for themselves." Education was a family affair, not just limited to the children. In almost all families, school children taught their parents at home.

> The desire for knowledge does not seem to have died away, as it was feared by many it would, after the novelty wore off. Some of our scholars have rarely lost a day, during three and a half years, except from sickness. Distance seems no barrier to the desire to learn.[38]

The following chart illustrates how much progress had been made from 1867 to 1870 in the South, but at the same time, it shows how much needed to be done:[39]

Year	Day and Night Schools	Teacher	Students
1867	1,382	1,641	89,234
1868	1,875	2,202	100,487
1869	1,961	2,267	96,332
1870	2,571	3,262	122,317

The bureau did not limit its activities to the establishment and support of common schools. In addition to providing leadership, buildings, and money for teachers' salaries, General O. O. Howard initiated a plan for the establishment of teacher training institutions. On May 4, 1867, Howard suggested that benevolent organizations develop a plan to establish normal schools and colleges for southern blacks. If the societies would provide the necessary leadership, he proposed to give them $50,000 in financial assistance. Over the next three years, Howard allocated $407,752 to twenty black higher educational institutions and $3,000 to a school for whites. By 1871, there were eleven colleges and universities established especially for the training of blacks. These schools provided the South with greatly needed trained teachers. Howard and the bureau did much to encourage this development.[40]

Howard University, named for General O. O. Howard, also improved. By 1870, the bureau reported that Howard University was assuming the character that its name implied. There were four hundred students in the academic and professional branches, plus an additional four hundred city residents who attended night classes. Howard then consisted of the following departments: normal, preparatory, collegiate, law, medical, theological, agricultural, military, commercial, musical, and night school (Lincoln Night School).[41]

Nevertheless, Howard was only one example of the successful results achieved by the bureau, blacks, and northern missionaries despite a hostile environment. Although parents were willing to deny opportunities to themselves in the interest of obtaining an education for their children, the need for income often required that children be absent from, or not attend school at all. The number of black schools and students in Alabama decreased due to lack of funds and increased violence. Lawless bands traveled throughout the South trying to suppress efforts to educate the freedmen. Alabama officials had unrealistically hoped that its freedmen schools would be self-reliant after three years, but extenuating circumstances—violence, crop failures, unsettled political affairs, and unemployment—ruined their plan.[42]

The Freedmen's Bureau did much to facilitate the education of black people, but it was not enough to compensate for hundreds of years of deprivation. What was even more unfortunate was the failure to aid the freedman at a time when their expectations were high and their need even higher. The federal government's refusal to sustain aid at a level to make a real difference caused two major problems for the freedmen. It meant that they had to rely on their own meager resources, which assured the race, as a whole, continued deprivation. The discontinuation of the bureau was a good indication to southerners that the federal government was placing in their hands responsibility for the Negro's welfare—especially their education. This abdication of responsibility for the education of blacks was a forerunner of the disastrous Hayes-Tilden Compromise in 1877 when the federal government in effect told the South that solving the "Negro problem" was a regional concern. Thus by default, the education of blacks was left primarily to the states, where the burden fell heavily upon the shoulders of blacks themselves.

Critics might argue that this position of the federal government was right and just, since education had always been a state and local responsibility. However, given the special slave status of the Negro, from which the group was so recently liberated, that group never should have been placed at the mercy of states and those individuals who had kept blacks in bondage so long. Justice and equality for blacks in all areas, including education, were not possible without federal assistance, monitoring, and enforcement. For the federal government to abdicate this clear responsibility, in view of the special circumstances of blacks, was a wanton dereliction of its responsibility.

EDUCATION OF BLACKS IN THE SOUTHERN STATES AFTER THE CIVIL WAR

The most important contribution made to educational opportunity during the Reconstruction era was the establishment of free, publicly supported education in the South, and this was due in large measure to the great appreciation and desire of black people for an education. During presidential Reconstruction, when southern conservative whites briefly gained control of their states, no thought was given to the education of the freedmen. Because of their great desire for an education, and as they gained political power, the freedmen concluded that the key to their advancement was education and saw the acquisition of knowledge as the remedy for their ills. They wanted not only education but integrated education. Segregation, the freedmen believed, violated the Fourteenth Amendment and made them unequal.[43]

W. E. B. DuBois concluded that in most southern states, the public school system *began* with the enfranchisement of blacks. In South Carolina, for example, the 1868 constitution, drawn up by blacks and their white radical allies, mentioned education for the first time in the history of the state. The constitution provided the outline of an educational system and obligated the

General Assembly to establish a system of universal education as soon as it was practical. No other item proposed by the constitutional convention aroused more opposition among white property holders, who felt that the tax burden would fall upon their shoulders.[44] They overlooked evidence to the contrary that blacks had labored all their lives for them, and that this was the least whites could do to compensate for slavery.

Yet, blacks continued in their struggle. They made public school attendance compulsory. A. J. Ransier, a black delegate to the convention, said: "I contend that in proportion to the education of the people so is their progress in civilization. Believing this, I believe that the committee has properly provided for the compulsory education of all children in this state between the ages named in the section [of the Constitution]." The black delegates also realized that whites wanted segregated facilities, but felt that schools should be provided for all; if some refused to attend, the fault was theirs.[45]

Blacks in other states either were more conciliatory or lacked the political power of blacks in South Carolina. In 1870 Georgia proposed to provide separate but equal schools for whites and blacks. In Alabama, a public school system was established by the constitution of 1867 and organized the following year. Reactionary whites were extremely vocal in their opposition to public education, but the demand for education was so great in the state that the conservative Democrats were forced to retain at least a remnant of the system in the new constitution of 1875. The Florida legislature in 1866 took a different course. It established a system of schools for blacks and stipulated that support of black schools had to come from blacks themselves. County schools were to be established only when the tax base was sufficient to support a school. After suffrage was extended to blacks, a law was passed in 1869 which established the first real public school system in the state. Jonathan C. Gibbs, a black former Secretary of State, was appointed Superintendent of Public Instruction in 1872. Under his leadership, Florida's pupil enrollment increased four-fold while expenses increased only 33 percent.[46]

Finances were the biggest problem for the new system. North Carolina was a case in point. The Reconstruction constitutional convention of 1868 and the state legislature of 1868-1869 established a fine system for the state, but poverty made its immediate realization impossible. The system also did not call for separate facilities for both races. In April 1869, the legislature authorized $100,000 for the system, to be raised primarily from the poll tax. There were 330,581 children between the ages of 6 and 21 in the state; 223,815 were white and 106,766 black.[47]

S. S. Ashly, a white northerner who favored mixed schools, was selected as superintendent, and under him was J. W. Hood, a subsequent Bishop of the A.M.E. Zion Church. Hood visited every section of the state in his efforts to compile a report on the status of education in North Carolina. His report indicated that the 106,766 blacks in the state were served by the 257 schools. These schools enrolled only 15,647 students. By the time the state began to make some improvements, the Democratic party had regained control. The state lost the services of Ashly and Hood who were replaced by Alexander McIver who in turn was succeeded by Stephen D. Pool. Pool promptly stole the financial aid provided by the Peabody Fund. The continued fear of mixed schools came to an end when the Democrats amended the constitution.[48]

Although blacks were not primary beneficiaries of public education, they did much to provide for its foundation. For the first time, in seven southern states constitutions were changed to allow state taxation for support of schools. Except for Alabama, this provision was retained in all the new constitutions that were revised by the Democrats. Democratic control often meant indifference and hostility to public education. State after state diverted money intended for the schools to other purposes, for whites considered the education of blacks useless and even dangerous to society. DuBois concluded that:

> The movement that saved the Negro public school system was not enlightened Southern opinion, but rather that Northern philanthropy which at the very beginning of the Negro education movement contributed toward the establishment of Negro colleges. The reason for them at first was to supply the growing demand for teachers, and was also a concession to Southern prejudice, which so violently disliked the white teacher in the Negro school.[49]

The northern missionaries in conjunction with blacks initially established the entire system of black higher education in the South. It was clear that the financial resources of private groups in the North were insufficient to support perpetually the black schools established throughout the region. With the withdrawal of the Freedmen's Bureau and finally federal troops, it was also evident that the federal government would not remain the protector of the former slaves. Thus, a system of Negro higher education had to be established to provide teachers for the primary schools already established.[50]

There were two important factors which affected the education of black people: whites continued to act upon their prejudice, and this action resulted in segregation and substantial lack of financial support at all levels. As shown before, the conservatives bitterly opposed universal education. They wanted to maintain, as closely as possible, the social order as it had been prior to the Civil War. They were opposed to all forms of education for blacks and were extremely hostile to any form of integrated education. During the 1870s, according to Professor Henry A. Bullock, a great detour occurred which sidetracked black education from that initially established by the missionaries to one which perpetuated the order of segregation. Bullock stated further that education for Negroes was limited to a "special" kind considered suitable to their status. Educational support for blacks was anchored not to a state's ability to fund it but to the whites' willingness to pay. Some whites opposed all forms of education for Negroes; some feared education would bring more federal intervention; some felt blacks were too inferior to learn; others, who ignored blacks' previous economic condition, felt that freedmen paid too few taxes to warrant educational expenditures. But whatever the feeling, black people had become strangers to whom the South felt it owed no obligation.[51]

White prejudice was transmitted into laws. As soon as conservative whites assumed control over state governments, state after state passed laws explicitly requiring segregated education. By 1877, segregated schools in the South were a *fait accompli*. There was also a growing movement led by Mississippi to provide more money for white education than was provided for black education. In 1886, Mississippi passed a teacher certification law which permitted separate salary scales for the two races; up to that time salaries were identical.[52]

Black public higher education was practically nonexistent prior to 1890. There were only two institutions that could be classified as a college or university in 1890; one had an enrollment of four college students and the other eighty-six. The thirteen public institutions of higher education were all classified as normal or industrial schools. The other public institutions which came into existence were founded after the passage of the Second Morrill Act in August 1890. The first Morrill Act was passed by Congress in 1863, and established land-grant institutions. It provided these institutions with annual appropriations of $15,000 each for the first year, rising each year by $1,000 until the maximum figure of $25,000 was reached. The key item relating to black education was the provision which stipulated that annual grants would be withheld from states which segregated blacks without providing separate agricultural and mechanical colleges for them. The law resulted in the establishment of seventeen black colleges in southern and border states. In general, these agricultural, mechanical, and industrial schools did not grant degrees.[53]

North Carolina, more progressive in its educational policy than most southern states, established a normal school for the training of black teachers. When Governor Zebulon Vance assumed the governorship in January 1877, he emphasized the need for training teachers. He proposed, and the legislature passed, a law which established two state normal schools, one for each race. The white normal school which was added to the university excluded blacks. The normal school for Negro teachers was established September 1877, at Fayetteville. Initially, there were forty students, but the number increased to fifty-eight, twenty of whom were female. By 1878, the number of students had increased to one hundred fourteen, and upon graduation students were required to teach in the public school system for a period of three years.[54]

The higher education of blacks in the North was not substantially better than that in the South. Two authors estimate that between 1865 and 1895 one hundred ninety-four blacks graduated from northern colleges, and of that number seventy-five graduated from Oberlin. Excluding Oberlin, the one hundred nineteen black graduates were distributed among fifty-two northern colleges, and averaged a little more than two graduates per college.[55] Thus, schools in the North, unencumbered by state law, did not markedly change their discriminatory admissions policies after the Civil War.

One can only conclude that the laws relating to the education of the freedmen in southern states did not facilitate equal education for blacks and whites, but encouraged continuing racial inequality. Further, the racial prejudices of southern inhabitants and legislators condoned segregated school systems and the meager financial support given for black education at all levels. The concept that blacks, if educated at all, should receive their education only at institutions suited to their alleged inferior capabilities, such as agricultural and vocational institutions, further blocked the attempts of blacks to acquire educational status equal to that of the white citizens.

Even after some progress had been made within the individual states, conditions in the South were generally poor, but worse for blacks. For the most part, progress for blacks occurred because of their own efforts and the Freedmen's Bureau and northern missionaries' assistance. The demise of the bureau was a serious blow to the effort by blacks to obtain an education, but even more serious was the retreat of the federal government. The government moved from a reluctant facilitator of black progress to a constructor of major legal barriers that culminated in the government giving legal sanction to segregation of the races.

The Supreme Court vs. Civil Rights for Blacks

The Fourteenth Amendment was passed by Congress and proposed to the states for adoption as a means of assuring that the Civil Rights Act of 1866 was not declared unconstitutional by the Supreme Court. In addition, the last section of each of the three Reconstruction amendments contained the provision which specified that Congress had the power to enforce the amendments by appropriate legislation. Nevertheless, the Supreme Court, between 1873 and 1883, handed down a series of major decisions that nullified the work of Congress during Reconstruction. These decisions curtailed the civil rights of black people and aided in the creation of the climate which led to the *Plessy* v. *Ferguson* decision of 1896—a decision which had disastrous consequences for black education.

The fear of a Supreme Court hostile to civil rights for blacks materialized in the *Slaughter House Cases* of 1873. Although the cases did not involve the rights of blacks as guaranteed under the carefully worked out "privileges and immunities," "due process," and "equal protection" clauses of the Fourteenth Amendment, the *Slaughter House Cases* nevertheless limited the effectiveness of the Fourteenth Amendment. The case itself involved the issue of whether an 1869 Louisiana law passed to regulate slaughter houses was constitutional when it gave a certain corporation a monopoly in maintaining slaughter houses in three Louisiana parishes.[56]

The nation was astounded by the Supreme Court decision after it reached the national tribunal. The Court held that there were still two categories of citizens—national and state. The privileges and immunities clause protected only those rights derived from national but not state citizenship. The Court basically repudiated the Fourteenth Amendment by narrowly defining federal citizenship rights to include all civil rights which were left to the state to protect. Since there were only a few rights which were derived from national citizenship, this removal of federal protection of the rights derived from state citizenship served as an effective barrier to the enforcement by the federal government of civil rights for blacks.[57]

Because of social violence and harassment of the freedmen, previously noted, Congress passed the Enforcement Act of 1870 and provided criminal sanctions for the citizen if two or more persons conspired to deny a citizen of his rights guaranteed by the Constitution. When a group of Louisiana whites broke up a political meeting of blacks in 1875, two of the whites were convicted, and their case came before the Supreme Court in *United States* v. *Cruikshank* (1876). The Court held that the rights of blacks as citizens were protected by the state. The decision also invalidated the Enforcement Act by ruling that the Fourteenth Amendment prohibited a state, not an individual, from denying its residents the equal protection of the law. The effect of the decision was tacitly to sanction the mob violence of the Ku Klux Klan in destroying the rights of blacks throughout the South. In effect, the states refused to protect the rights of blacks while the Supreme Court refused to allow Congress to do so.[58]

During the same term, the Court released another decision in *United States* v. *Reese*. The case involved the refusal of an election official to review and count the black vote in a state election. The indictments were based on the third and fourth sections of the Enforcement Act which prohibited persons from refusing to count votes for reasons of race or color. These sections did not state "race or color," as in the first two sections, but added instead "as aforesaid." The court used this judicial pettifoggery to forestall the work of Congress and invalidate another piece of legislation designed to enforce the provisions of the Fourteenth Amendment. In *United States* v. *Harris* (1883), Section 2 of the Enforcement Act of 1871 was declared unconstitutional, in spite of the government's arguments that Congress had a right and duty to act when the states failed to take affirmative action to protect their citizens in the exercise of their rights.[59]

The Civil Rights Act of 1875,* as noted previously, was the last civil rights act passed by Congress during the nineteenth century. The bill prohibited discrimination in public accommodations excluding churches, cemeteries, and public schools. The act provided for not less than $500 fine or fines and imprisonment for offenders. The act underscored the belief that the due process and equal protection clauses gave Congress the authority to protect constitutional rights of the people when the states refused to do so. When a constitutional test of the act finally reached the Supreme Court in the *Civil Rights Cases* of 1883, Reconstruction had ended, federal troops had been withdrawn from the South, and the egalitarianism of previous years had subsided.[60]

Five cases involving the denial of public accommodations were combined in the *Civil Rights Cases*. The three cases which were indicative of the pervasiveness of discrimination came respectively from the Northwest, a border state, and the South. The cases were brought on the grounds that racial discrimination was a badge of servitude, which the Thirteenth Amendment

---

*The Act was almost identical to the Civil Rights Act of 1964, which would follow it by almost a hundred years.

was designed to eliminate, and that the amendment gave Congress power to enforce it. But the Court ruled that the Thirteenth Amendment was inapplicable; that the Fourteenth Amendment forbade discriminatory actions by the states, not by individuals. Sections 1 and 2 were declared unconstitutional.[61] Justice John Harlan gave his lone dissent:

> The opinion in these cases proceeds, it seems to me, upon grounds entirely too narrow and artificial. I can not resist the conclusion that the substance and spirit of the recent Amendment of the Constitution have been sacrificed by a subtle and ingenious verbal criticism.
>
> I am of the opinion that such discrimination practiced by corporations and individuals in the exercise of their public or quasi-public functions is a badge of servitude the imposition of which Congress may prevent under its power, by appropriate legislation, to enforce the Thirteenth Amendment; and, consequently, without reference to its enlarged Power under the Fourteenth Amendment, the Act of March 1, 1875, is not in my judgement, repugnant to the Constitution.[62]

The Supreme Court, over a ten-year period, virtually nullified the legislation passed during the era of Reconstruction. Not only was the legislation inadequate in providing equality to blacks, but the laws had not been rigorously enforced. By declaring the laws, or portions of it, unconstitutional, the Court effectively removed what little protection existed for blacks in a hostile environment. Despite the Reconstruction amendments, the Court, through its decisions, permitted the continuation of racial segregation and discrimination throughout the nation. The nation not only had abandoned blacks but also had paved the way for the long era of Jim Crow and the political nadir of black people.

Jim Crowism and Black Education Sidetracked

As the century neared a close, it was more and more evident that neither the federal government nor the states were willing to provide the type of affirmative action programs necessary to prepare blacks for the conditions facing them as free persons. Instead of providing special assistance, the nation tired of "waving the bloody shirt" and witnessing the animosity that continued between the two regions. Racial attitudes obviously had not changed; most whites still believed that blacks were inferior and therefore should be separated as much as possible from the dominant group. The seeds of Negro second-class citizenship and special education were sown during this period. Since blacks were viewed as inferior, and business interest required a cheap labor supply, black education was sidetracked into special education so blacks could be suitably trained for their place in southern society.

Northern economic concerns were indifferent to the political and economic interests of black people; blacks, as a result, were reduced to a state of peonage, and their education was developed accordingly. Capitalists were reluctant to invest in the South following the Civil War. Northern banking houses initially limited their investments to railroads and state bonds. The old rail system was rebuilt and an additional 8,000 miles of track were added to the existing system. (The 1873 depression halted construction temporarily, but by 1880 the South had a total of twenty thousand miles of track which served as a communication link uniting the South with the North.)[63] Although the repudiation of state debts after Reconstruction aroused doubt of the trustworthiness of the South's fiscal policies, northern and southern businessmen worked together when economic interests were mutually beneficial.

Northern financiers soon learned that disruptive race relations were not conducive to good business, but instead of using their influence to assure some measure of equality for blacks, they succumbed to racism. As blacks regressed from poor tenant farmers to a state of peonage, they were eventually denied most civil rights. The "Negro problem" ceased to be an element of sectional controversy, and race relations moved from a state of chaotic ambivalence to a rigid class structure, resembling in many ways a slave society. Although the system allowed some blacks who owned property to rise, the number of blacks who owned a significant amount of property was minimal. The system itself required a degree of education for black people, and it was within this sphere that a meeting of the minds occurred between the North and the South. A compromise was reached on Hampton's industrial education which served as a bridge for better understanding between the two regions. George Peabody, who made a fortune in wholesale drygoods, established the Peabody Education Fund in 1867 to promote education in the South. Though with benevolent intent, agents of the fund, in essence, actively encouraged blacks to seek a second-class education.[64]

Education for black people, as it developed in the South, was a result of southern racism backed by northern money. After the war, there were two schools of thought on the best type of education for blacks. One believed that industrial education was best suited for the Negro, while the other felt a liberal arts education patterned after the New England schools was more suited to the needs of black people. Northern missionaries and teachers who came South during the Reconstruction era were some of the best educated in the nation's common school system and New England's colleges and universities. They came South with missionary zeal to work among the freedmen and endured the hardships, as well as the brutal treatment from southern whites. They believed that freedom for the Negro meant that he must be in a position to care for himself and participate in a free society like other people. The missionaries held no misconceptions about the Negro's ability to learn, and they taught in the same manner as they had been taught in New England. Negroes demonstrated their ability to learn and were willing to endure the hardships necessary to achieve an education. The hardships were many; teachers and students frequently saw their efforts turn to ashes as whites burned school-houses and beat school teachers.[65]

These missionaries soon realized the Negroes' need for higher education. There were not enough northern educators to fulfill the need for teachers; even they would not remain in the South forever. The answer was to train black teachers. More black colleges were needed to meet the growing demand. The American Missionary Association established Fisk University in 1865 in Nashville, Tennessee and Talladega College in Talladega, Alabama. The same year Atlanta University was inaugurated under very difficult circumstances. The American Baptist Home Mission Society formed Richmond Theological Seminary and helped establish Morehouse College and Shaw University among others.[66]

Unlike the northern missionaries, General S. C. Armstrong, founder of Hampton Normal and Agricultural Institute for Negro Youth in 1868, believed that racial differences required normal schools for blacks. Armstrong thought that blacks could acquire knowledge, but lacked the ability to assimilate and digest it. The philosophy of vocational education for blacks, which eventually gained southern and northern support, was established early and perpetuated by Booker T. Washington, one of Armstrong's students at Hampton.[67]

Armstrong's programs for Negro education approximated what southern whites felt was best for black people, and his plan found general acceptance throughout the South, especially after the turn of the century. The Peabody Fund did much to bring about this occurrence.

Although George Peabody established the fund, Dr. Barnas Sears, former President of Brown University and Secretary of the Massachusetts

Board of Education, was the fund's first agent; under his leadership a policy for the fund was established. Through selective funding, this policy influenced the course of education in the South. Sears was opposed to interracial education and refused to allocate funds to mixed schools or school systems. When Louisiana, during the Reconstruction years, established a mixed school system, which was a constant source of irritation for whites in the state, Dr. Sears denied Lousiana Peabody money because he felt that there was a lack of white support for the interracial schools. The other provision of Sears's policy was to grant funds on the condition that a larger amount would be raised by taxation. The policy was designed to develop a sound base for education in the South, but the money was limited. The fund seldom granted more than $90,000 a year, and only the larger towns and cities could raise the necessary matching funds. Between 1868 and 1914, the largest grant to any one state was $37,975, given to Virginia in 1874. It is notable that in North Carolina, where the citizens struggled to establish a viable system of education, the fund provided assistance, but not at the level needed. In 1869, the fund gave the state $6,350. By 1871, the amount had increased to $8,750, but fell to $8,250 the following year.[68]

Sears died in 1880 and was replaced by Jabez Lamar Monroe Curry, who was agent for the fund until 1903. Curry, born and educated in the South, identified with the governing class that favored secession over abolition of slavery. After the war, he thought it prudent to advocate education for blacks. Having taken over as agent, he traveled widely throughout the South in the interest of promoting southern education. Curry did not believe that the schools could solve the most difficult of social problems, but he did feel that "it [education] could promote prosperity, alleviate racial friction, and help to resolve the conflict between capital and labor." Because Curry perceived economic and cultural conflicts of the Reconstruction era, he saw the overthrow of white-black rule as a victory for the South. But once conservatives were restored to power, Curry used his influence to reconcile the two sections.[69]

In line with new industry that began to move into the South, Curry advocated the incorporation of industrial education into the southern school system. He thought that vocational education for whites and blacks was the best way to achieve economic prosperity. Like other southerners, he assumed that white supremacy was not only inevitable but desirable. Curry saw enfranchisement as a great blunder. He was not impressed by the achievement of a few blacks who had received the opportunity for an education. He concluded that education would do very little to improve the conditions of the race as a whole. Nevertheless, to his credit, Curry did encourage southerners to provide education for blacks and spoke out against laws that allowed only Negro taxes to support Negro schools. He also spoke out against the lynchings so prevalent throughout the South.[70]

The impact Armstrong, Sears, and Curry had on the subsequent education of black people, an education that was sidetracked from that proposed by northern missionaries, was formidable. A firm precedent prior to the turn of the century was established: these men and other advocates of black education proposed a type of training that would accommodate black people's second-class position in southern society. Their belief in black inferiority led them to promote vocational education. This overemphasis on industrial education for blacks impeded the overall educational advancement and subsequent social, political, and economic progress of the race. The foundation for the inferior education of the Negro was firmly established prior to 1890. The decades preceding and following 1900 were the years in which black people were unmitigatedly entrenched into second-class citizenship, and not until the post-World War II years were efforts made which substantially reversed this process.

BLACK PEOPLE, EDUCATION AND THE AGE OF JIM CROW, 1890-1915

SECOND CLASS CITIZENSHIP FOR BLACK AMERICANS

The turn of the century marked the political nadir of black people in America. As long as some blacks continued to exercise the franchise, southern whites felt threatened. Only by restoring to rampant racism was the South able to unite and effectively eliminate the Negro from the political arena. The process began with the revision of state constitutions and statutes. What could not be legally achieved was accomplished through violence and intimidation—actions very similar to the procedure whites used to overthrow Reconstruction. The effort to make blacks second-class citizens received official federal sanctions in the infamous *Plessy* v. *Ferguson* decision, which stunned the black community.

Southern whites assumed that blacks were inferior and a source of cheap labor, and that political power was the province solely of the white race. Since blacks were declared inferior there was little need, it was reasoned, to provide them with an education; any education provided was designed to ensure that blacks fit into the emerging class structure. Anxious to maintain good relations with the "new South," influential northerners aided and abetted this whole process. In an effort to rescue what he could from an intolerable situation, Booker T. Washington's philosophy compounded the problem. As a result, blacks, and particularly education for blacks, suffered. The damage was so great that not even the *Brown* decision of 1954 came close to eradicating the generations of deprivation.

The years from 1890 to 1954 illustrate how race prejudice and discrimination were institutionalized in spite of constitutional provisions for equal citizenship. The resultant damage can only be rectified through a reversal of discrimination, or minimally, the institutionalization of affirmative action efforts to bring blacks into the mainstream of American society. What black people accomplished during this period was achieved in spite of the system and because of their overriding faith in education as a means of self-improvement.

Law and Disorder

Professor Rayford W. Logan classified 1890-1900 as ten years which marked the greatest victories won by the South since the compromise of 1877. At the national level two important bills were defeated. In 1890, the Senate rejected a bill to aid public education. Senator Blair from New Hampshire introduced a plan in which the federal government would give assistance to state public school systems over a period of eight years. The allocations were to be based on the proportion of illiterates in a state over ten years to the total number of illiterates nationwide. States that maintained separate school systems were to divide the funds, if they discriminated between white and black. The provision, of course, excluded segregation as a form of discrimination. Southern reaction to the bill was mixed. They recognized the need for federal assistance because they felt that the South should not have to bear the responsibility for educating the Negro alone. Curry, agent for the Peabody Fund, actively lobbied for the bill. But the South's politicians were unwilling to accept the bill without conditions. They feared that it might lead to federal intervention into southern affairs. The bill was defeated by the combined vote of Republicans and southern Democrats.[1]

That same year Henry Cabot Lodge of Massachusetts introduced a bill to provide for federal supervision of federal elections. Although it clearly did not provide for the use of force, opponents of the bill quickly dubbed it the "force bill." Dr. Logan contends that the debates in the House clearly indicated that southerners and even some northern whites were determined that the South should continue to handle the Negro question without the interference of the federal government. After a hot debate the bill, which was voted almost strictly along party lines, was defeated. Now the right of

Negroes to vote was no longer a constitutional issue, but had become a political question.[2]

The national government clearly was unwilling to act in behalf of blacks in the South. This inactivity spurred southern Democrats to finish the task of "restoration" left incomplete since Reconstruction. Six weeks after the failure of the Lodge bill, the Mississippi Constitutional Convention convened August 12, 1890, with an overwhelming Democratic majority and one lone Negro, Isaiah T. Montgomery. The intent of the convention was to eliminate the black vote—even though 56.9 percent of the state population was black. The convention approved the new constitution on November 1, 1890, after adopting the report of the judiciary committee that it was not necessary to submit the changes to the people for approval. The constitution provided for a poll tax of two dollars, excluded certain convicted criminals from the franchise, and imposed a literacy test in which a potential voter had to read and understand certain sections of the state constitution. The revised constitution was a clear attempt to nullify the Fifteenth Amendment to the United States Constitution. It also violated the provision whereby Mississippi was readmitted to the Union. The state had pledged that its constitution would never be revised to deprive any United States citizen who was entitled to vote under the 1868 Constitution of the right to vote, except in the case of punishment for a felony.[3]

It was becoming more and more obvious that the American Creed did not apply to black people. After the defeat of the Lodge Bill, the Republicans, under President Harrison, for all practical purposes abandoned their efforts to protect the constitutional rights of blacks. Further, no action was taken on an anti-lynching bill at a time when more and more blacks were being lynched. The following numbers of persons were lynched from 1882 to 1892, most of whom were black:[4]

Year	Number
1882	113
1883	130
1884	211
1885	184
1886	138
1887	120
1888	137
1889	170
1890	96
1891	184

Compared to earlier times, northern reaction to the disfranchisement of blacks in Mississippi was mild, and there was generally no serious effort to intervene in Mississippi's internal affairs.[5] Thus it was clear which way the South was moving, and even clearer that the North was willing to allow the South to suppress blacks and push them into second or even third-class citizenship.

Within this climate arose Booker T. Washington, a man who climbed to the pinnacle of Negro leadership. Washington was born a slave in Virginia in 1856, son of a white father and slave mother in Franklin County, Virginia. Following the Civil War, his mother took him to Malden, West Virginia, where he was not a stranger to poverty. Early in life, Washington worked during the day and attended school at night. While working as a servant in the home of a mine owner, he learned of Hampton Institute in Virginia. In 1872, at the age of sixteen, Washington left Malden, West Virginia with $1.50 to take the 500-mile trip to Hampton. Washington's entrance examination consisted of sweeping the recitation room. On that basis alone, Booker T. Washington was admitted to Hampton Institute and immediately came under the influence of General Samuel C. Armstrong.[6]

Washington wrote that Armstrong made a lasting impression on him and that he was "the noblest, rarest human being that it has ever been my privilege to meet." While president of Hampton Institute, Armstrong impressed upon his students the value of labor, especially skilled labor, and how such values form and build character. In addition, he insisted that education had to be won rather than awarded. Armstrong wanted to train Negro youth who in turn could go out and teach their people and lead them by example. He thought that industrial education would not only provide self-support, but would also build the character of the race. He placed great emphasis on lifting labor out of the arena of drudgery into meaningful work that required skill and thought. Armstrong believed that industrial education for the Negro would bring the two races together, with black people providing the skills whites needed.[7]

Washington incorporated the teachings and philosophy of Armstrong into his personal belief and life. He graduated from Hampton in 1875 and returned to Malden to teach in the same school he had attended as a young man. He enrolled in Wayland Seminary in Washington, D.C. in 1878. After a year at Wayland, he left and took a position as instructor at Hampton. In 1881, upon the recommendation of General Armstrong, Washington took the job of establishing a normal school for black teachers in Tuskegee, Alabama. His travels reinforced his belief in industrial education for black people. In his autobiography, Washington commented that the worst thing he saw during his travels, was a young man living in filth and studying French grammar.[8]

As Washington began more and more to articulate what the southern and northern whites wanted to hear, his influence also increased. In 1884, Washington spoke to the National Education Association stating that the future of blacks in the United States depended upon their ability to develop skills and character that would make them indispensable to the surrounding community. In 1885, he was elected president of the Alabama State Teachers Association. A portion of the black press joined Washington in advocating industrial education for blacks while belittling higher education. A writer in the February 18, 1882 edition of *The People's Advocate* in Washington, D.C. suggested that blacks were not ready for formal academic training and that permanent equality would occur only after sufficient industrial training.[9]

Washington's emphasis on industrial education and conciliation with whites was undoubtedly an important reason why he was invited to speak at the Cotton States and International Exposition, September 18, 1895. His speech brought him national fame and secured his place as a national spokesman for black people. He was determined not to say anything to offend whites while trying to be true to his own people. Washington began by pointing out that one-third of the people in the South were colored, and if the South was to progress they could not be ignored. He suggested that blacks should cast down their buckets where they were and make friends with whites. He proposed that they learn agriculture, mechanics, commerce, domestic service, and professions. Washington warned that blacks had to begin at the bottom and not at the top.[10]

Washington then turned to the whites in the audience and urged them to use black labor as opposed to relying upon immigrant labor. He pointed out that blacks had not used the strike or carried out labor wars and could be depended upon. He then added, "In all things that are purely social we can be as separate as the fingers, yet one as the hand in all things essential to mutual progress." The crowd applauded frantically in response. Washington further added that the wisest blacks realize that through struggle the race will progress, but to raise the question of social equality is extremist folly. Washington did not ignore the Negro's right to legal privileges, but indicated that it was vastly more important that Negroes be prepared to exercise those privileges. When Washington completed his speech he had accepted a subordinate position for black people in southern society, and in return, he asked that blacks be given the opportunity to earn a decent living. The southern press placed great emphasis on his renunciation of social equality.[11]

The South did not hesitate to show Washington its friendly face. In the fall of the same year, the South Carolina Constitutional Convention was in session to disfranchise blacks. After Wade Hampton was elected governor following Reconstruction, he failed to keep his promise that he would provide protection for the Negro in the state. At the same time, he did not completely eliminate the Negro from politics, although the Negro's participation steadily declined from 1876 to 1890. Following Hampton's defeat by Ben Tillman, Tillman proclaimed during his inauguration that whites would be supreme in the state. The legislature failed to carry through such proposals as segregated railroads (already segregated by the railroads themselves) and demands for a constitutional convention to disfranchise blacks. Only after the Populist movement had gained some strength during the elections of 1894 and had become a threat to Democratic rule, was Tillman able to push through, just a few months after Washington's address, his constitutional amendment which disfranchised most of the state's blacks.[12]

In Alabama, Washington's state, the law had been revised in 1891 to allow local authorities to distribute school funds. The distribution was so inequitable that figures were not published until 1908, by which time blacks had been so completely disfranchised that any protest made was meaningless. The following chart illustrates the inequities in one black belt Alabama County.[13]

	White Children	Black Children	Total Salaries for White Teachers	Total Salaries for Black Teachers
1890-91	2,482	9,931	$ 4,397	$6,545
1907-08	2,285	10,745	$28,108	$3,940

The chart illustrates very graphically what whites meant by friendly relations. They would remain friendly as long as blacks stayed in their place. To assure that they remained in their place the legal system was changed to force them into, and the educational system changed to teach them, just what their place would be. The stage was set. The South elevated a prominent black to a position of national leadership after he accepted what the South perceived to be total acquiescence to Negro second-class citizenship. What impact Booker T. Washington had on the Supreme Court remains speculative, but the following year the Court sanctioned segregation and, in effect, second-class citizenship for black people.

Plessy v. Ferguson (1896) and Its Impact on Blacks

The case arose when Homer Adolph Plessy, one-eighth black and seven-eighths white, refused to ride in the "colored" car on a railroad train during a trip within the state of Louisiana. He was arrested and charged with violating the 1890 Louisiana law which required separate but equal facilities for both races. Plessy filed suit and charged that the act violated the Thirteenth and Fourteenth Amendments. Years earlier the Louisiana Supreme Court had ruled that the law violated the Constitution when applied to interstate passengers. Hiring a New York lawyer, Albion W. Tourgee, Louisiana blacks took the case before the Supreme Court.[14]

Justice Brown delivered the opinion of the Court. The Court found that the Louisiana law was not in conflict with the Thirteenth and Fourteenth Amendments because a state statute which provided for legal distinction— based upon the fact of color—did not destroy the legal equality of the two races. The Fourteenth Amendment did not intend "to enforce absolute equality of the two races before the law, and to enforce comingling of the two races," and it could not have eliminated distinctions based on race. Laws permitting or even requiring separation do not necessarily imply inferiority, the Court held. As an example, the Court cited the outdated and inapplicable Massachusetts Supreme Court decision upholding the right of the Boston School Committee to provide for separate instruction of black children. The question in the view of the Court rested, therefore, on whether the Louisiana law was reasonable. The Court ruled that it was.[15]

Once again Justice Harlan issued his resounding dissent. Aside from the apparent injustice of the Louisiana law, Justice Harlan concluded that it was not consistent with the United States Constitution because the Thirteenth Amendment does not allow any burden or disability to be imposed as a badge of slavery. Justice Harlan went on to quote the Fourteenth Amendment wherein "no state shall make or enforce any law which shall abridge the privileges or immunities of citizens of the United States; nor shall any state deprive any person of life, liberty or property without due process of law, or deny to any person within its judisdiction the equal protection of the laws."[16]

It was clear to Justice Harlan that if these two amendments were enforced according to their meaning and intent, the civil rights of all Americans would be secured. He concluded that American institutions were based upon "the broad and sure foundations of the equality of all men before the law. . . ." Therefore, he had to dissent from the majority decision.[17]

Not since the abolition of slavery had a decision made such a severe and

negative impact on black education. Taking their cue from the *Plessy* decision, southern states, using the sanction of law, began to impose a series of
political, civil, economic, and social restrictions on blacks. State after state
rewrote its constitution and implemented statutes to legally formalize patterns
of segregation and discrimination. So strongly did Louisiana whites feel
about suppressing black people that they incorporated in their state constitution provisions to negate the Fourteenth and Fifteenth Amendments.[18]

The right to vote was made extremely complicated in the 1898 Louisiana
constitution in order to eliminate the black vote, while still allowing often less
qualified whites to vote. All voters had to be able to read and write; but if
unable to do so, they could qualify if they possessed property valued at not
less than three hundred dollars. The article further stipulated that unless the
male of voting age had voted prior to 1867, or was the son or grandson of such
a voter, he could not qualify to vote. This particular provision was popularly
known as the "grandfather clause" and was one of the most devious tools
used to deny blacks the vote. The major section of the article prescribed a poll
tax of one dollar per annum to be paid before a person could vote.[19] The
constitution was written to progressively eliminate blacks as a political factor
in the state. Those few who could read and meet the property qualification
were probably eliminated by the grandfather clause. Since conservative
whites were in control of the state prior to Radical Reconstruction, it is
extremely unlikely that they knowingly permitted blacks to vote. Just for
good measure, the poll tax was added to further assure a lack of black
participation in the political process.

Louisiana was but one example of a process that occurred throughout the
South. These states used the grandfather clause, poll tax, the white primary,
and understanding clause to the constitution and other means, or various
combinations of them, to disfranchise blacks. As the number of blacks
increased in urban areas, there was a steady demand for increased segregation. Laws were passed to segregate blacks in public accommodations,
transportation, waiting rooms, ticket windows, drinking fountains, restaurants, factories, and residential areas. Even the executive branch of the federal
government sanctioned Jim Crowism when President Woodrow Wilson permitted segregation in government offices in Washington.[20]

To enforce the legal restrictions placed on black people, whites again
resorted to extralegal tactics to control them. Klan activities increased, as well
as subsequent brutality and cruelty to blacks. From 1901 to 1910, there were
754 lynchings, 90 percent of which took place in the South. Neither Congress,
the President nor state governments took any action to prevent or curtail these

lynchings, even when they were publicized in advance. Large-scale rioting also increased, both in the North and South. Violent acts against blacks culminated in the Atlanta Massacre of September 22, 1906, in which scores of whites roved the city, looting, murdering, and lynching blacks.[21]

While defining the legal status of blacks in a white supremacist society, southerners did not overlook education. The Tennessee Act of March 13, 1901 is a typical example of segregationist statutes enacted throughout the South. Unlike the Louisiana constitution of 1898, which attempted to achieve its end through subterfuge, the Tennessee Act was blunt and unequivocal. The act read:

> An act to prohibit the co-education of the white and colored races and to prohibit the white and colored races from attending the same schools, academies, colleges, or other places of learning in this state.
>
> Section 1. Be it enacted by the General Assembly of the State of Tennessee, That hereafter it shall be unlawful for any school, academy, college or other place of learning to allow white and colored persons to attend the same school, academy, college or other place of learning.
>
> Section 2. Be it further enacted, That it shall be unlawful for any teacher, professor or educator in the State, in any college, academy or school of learning, to allow the white and colored races to attend the same school, or for any teacher or educator, or other person to instruct or teach both the white and colored races in the same class, school or college building, or in any other place of learning, or allow or permit the same to be done with their knowledge, consent, or procurement.
>
> Section 3. Be it further enacted, That any person or persons violating this Act or any of its provisions, when convicted shall be fined for each offense fifty ($50) dollars and imprisoned not less than thirty days nor more than six months, at the discretion of the Court.
>
> Section 4. Be it further enacted, That Grand Juries shall have inquisitorial powers of all violations of the Act, and the same to be given in charge Circuit Court Judges to the Grand Juries.
>
> Section 5. Be it further enacted, That this Act shall take effect from and after the first day of September, 1901, the public welfare requiring it. Approved March 13, 1901.[22]

Such provisions were not uncommon or unexpected. Southern states had received notification in the *Plessy* decision that the Supreme Court sanctioned the idea of separate but equal in railroad transportation. But the Court went further. In *Cummings* v. *County Board of Education* (1899), the Court by implication had accepted the provision of segregated education for whites and blacks.[23] It was only a matter of time before all states proceeded to adopt the separate but equal doctrine in their body of laws.

Segregation enforced by law was not limited to primary and secondary education, and the states went so far as to compel, not only their public institutions of higher education, but even private schools that attempted to provide education for both races, to segregate. Berea College had continuously, except for the Civil War years, provided an education for black and white low income students. The experiment was quite successful, and it did not seem to matter to the students which race was in the majority. By the turn of the century, Berea College was the only institution of higher education in Kentucky which maintained an integrated student body. In 1904, the Kentucky legislature passed a law barring the teaching of white and black students on the same campus. The school appealed the decision first to the Kentucky Supreme Court, which upheld the statute. The case appeared before the Supreme Court in 1908 as *Berea College* v. *Kentucky*. The Court accepted the Kentucky law which banned private schools from admitting black and white students to the same campus. Berea College complied and established Lincoln Institute near Louisville, Kentucky for its black students. Unfortunately for them, the top level administrators and staff remained at the original campus and established a Hampton-type program for the black students at Lincoln.[24]

What southern whites had not achieved by the end of Reconstruction had been achieved by the end of the nineteenth century and the beginning of the twentieth century. After it was evident that the national government would no longer interfere in the internal affairs of the southern states, racism and discrimination became rampant. The movement to disfranchise blacks increased to the point where blacks were completely eliminated as a political force in the South. The political repression was followed by enforced segregation condoned by the highest court in the land, and Booker T. Washington was elevated to the position of spokesman for black people because of his willingness to subjugate political aspirations in favor of economic progress; this progress to be achieved through industrial education.

What Washington failed to realize was that without political power or influence, black people had no means to protect themselves. The gains blacks achieved were only as stable as their ability to protect their holdings in the political arena. It was obvious from the number of lynchings which occurred that whites were intolerant of any dissent, and any leader who departed from the accepted mode of behavior could anticipate mob violence and even death. Further, by overemphasizing industrial education to the detriment of liberal arts education, the South was free to proceed with its plan to educate black people to conform to white supremist society. Thus, in the words of Henry A. Bullock, education became general for whites in the South and special for blacks.

Special Education for Negroes

The last quarter of the nineteenth century ensnared the Negro in economic and social movements beyond his control. The growth of industrialism in the South and the rise of southern politicians favorable to northern economic interest eliminated the need for Republican dependence on the black vote. Hence, the Republican Congress in 1890 defeated the Lodge Federal Election Bill and the Blair Federal Aid to Education Bill, which would have protected black political rights and improved both black and white schools in the South.[25]

American expansionism, or imperialism, abroad served to reinforce racism at home. Southerners did not overlook the significance of America's exploitation of colored people in foreign lands such as in the Philippines and Puerto Rico. To southerners, there appeared to be a tacit approval of their own race relations when the federal government issued its policy of Oriental exclusion. Even social Darwinism, in vogue at the time, was used to justify the mistreatment of black people.[26]

Since the Republican Party and northern capitalists no longer needed to depend upon the Negro vote, they became more interested in maintaining a stable labor supply and exploiting southern resources than in protecting Negro rights. The romance between agrarian reformers and black people was short-lived. During the struggle between the Populists and finance capitalism, blacks were among the losers. They were used as the scapegoats for the difficulties of the white working and small farmer class.[27]

Thus, during this period, 1894-1915, while white Americans were attempting to find what place black Americans would assume in the society, black men and women probably experienced more oppression than at any other time since slavery. Within this atmosphere of crime and violence, the philosophy of Negro education was taking shape. The theory of Negro education, as it developed at the turn of the century, reflected the status of the blacks in the larger community.

By 1894, the idea of special education for Negroes had taken hold and begun to challenge the image of classical education set by earlier northern missionaries and teachers. General Armstrong of Hampton Institute believed that blacks had developed a distaste for labor during slavery and that it was now important to show them the dignity of labor through industrial education, which would open opportunities for them in agriculture and mechanical, industrial, and domestic work. Negroes would then be self-supporting and the South would be provided with a labor force of great potential wealth. Although there was some disagreement with Armstrong's ideas, whites, both North and South, agreed that Negroes should be trained in accordance with their status in American life.[28]

Little support for Negro higher education existed in the South prior to the passage of the Second Morrill Act of 1890. The first act, passed in 1862, established federal support for higher education in the form of land-grant colleges. The second act provided schools with annual appropriations of $15,000 each for the first year, rising each year by $1,000 until the maximum of $25,000 was reached. The key to the development of black colleges was the provision in the bill which stipulated that annual grants be withheld from states which segregated blacks without providing separate agricultural and mechanical colleges for them. Thus, the law resulted in the establishment of seventeen black colleges, mainly nondegree-granting agricultural, mechanical, and industrial schools.[29]

Until the Supreme Court sanctioned the South's dual school system, there was little difference in the financial support given to black and white schools. Schools were opened relatively the same number of days and teachers paid about the same. As the educational system grew, the strain on the southern tax system began to appear. School officials began to seek ways to divert money from the Negro schools in order to reduce school taxes or increase appropriations for white students. Most states adopted laws to allow local boards to use state money as they saw fit. No objective criteria were provided for the separate but equal doctrine. Since blacks had been disfranchised, they had lost the one tool necessary to assure them quality education. Whites conveniently rationalized that the type of education Negroes needed was less expensive than that needed for white students. They reasoned that since Negroes were farmers, mechanics, and domestics, their education should be designed to make them perform these tasks more efficiently.[30]

The result was the development of a special education system for blacks which was designed to prepare Negroes for their special position within a caste structure in the South. This type of system was supported by the government structure, and blatantly discriminated against and handicapped blacks at all levels. It completely separated them from whites without cross-fertilization, which is so necessary for a progressive system. Teachers were trained who had fewer qualifications than their white counterparts. They worked in leaky, poorly constructed schools; there were often no desks—just backless benches and a few tattered books—and the school year could begin only when the crops had been harvested. Under these conditions, it was just short of a miracle what these schools achieved. Whites conveniently used the self-fulfilling prophecy: Negroes could not learn and, therefore, they were deprived of the financial support necessary to acquire an adequate education.[31]

Special education for Negroes was meant to be more than industrial; it was designed to be a way of life—a way to perpetuate a caste condition. The plan was to isolate blacks socially from whites by a rigid system of residential segregation. They were to be limited to special jobs by means of employment discrimination. Tailored in Negro ways through a rigid code of interracial etiquette, these attitudes were to be reinforced by their obedience to caste rules through their formal education.[32]

With the advice of Booker T. Washington and leading southern white men, various philanthropic organizations did much to shape the special character of black education. Whereas the Peabody Fund had for a number of years assisted Negro schools as well as others in the South, the John F. Slater Fund moved boldly into the area of helping to improve the Negro elementary and secondary schools in the rural areas. Philanthropists also helped Negro colleges, which depended upon outside assistance for their survival. Because of the outstanding work of Hampton and Tuskegee Institutes in the area of industrial education, these schools received the largest gifts from the fund. The Slater Fund's policy in education crystalized around teacher training and industrial education. During the 1905-1906 school year, the fund contributed $40,000 to eighteen Negro colleges throughout the South. The money was primarily designated for the development and maintenance of industrial departments. Liberal arts colleges established to train ministers, teachers, and even doctors found that a large part of the funds they received went to pay the salaries of teachers who taught cooking and sewing.[33]

Washington's influence stimulated other northern philanthropists to move into the area of Negro education. Washington encouraged John D. Rockefeller to establish the General Education Board in 1902, and also played a part in the development of the Anna T. Jeanes Fund, the Phelps-Stokes Fund, and the Rosenwald Rural School program. A large portion of their contributions went to Washington's Tuskegee Institute, but every area of black education in the South was affected by the work of these funds.[34]

Washington suggested to the various educators and philanthropists that Negroes needed a particular kind of education for their particular condition. Washington did not need to persuade the boards of trustees and their agents. They just followed the pattern established thirty years earlier by the seg-regationist agent of the Peabody Fund who consistently recommended that black recipients should receive less money than whites since "it costs less to maintain schools for colored children than whites." By the turn of the century, agents for the various philanthropic organizations then in existence, and others which followed, believed that they should work within the south-ern system and try to improve the Negro's lot within the limits defined by southern whites. These agents differed from earlier northern missionaries, who believed that they *should* accomplish what *should* be done; the agents of secular philanthropies believed that they *should* accomplish what they thought *could* be done. As a result, improvement in Negro education was painfully slow.[35]

Yet, there were some accomplishments. In 1907 the Anna T. Jeanes Foundation was established for the purpose of improving black schools. In her will Anna T. Jeanes established the fund with a $1 million endowment and appointed Booker T. Washington and Hollis Burke Frissel of Hampton Institute, among others, to serve on the board. The fund was to be used for the assistance of rural, community, or county schools for southern Negroes. The money was not for the benefit or use of large institutions, but for the purpose of providing basic education. At the first meeting of the board on February 29, 1908, Booker T. Washington was unanimously elected chairman. Other members of the board included Andrew Carnegie, Robert R. Moton, James H. Dillard, and Robert L. Smith. The policy established by the board included the following:

1.   That the general educational situation should be studied carefully;
2.   That any work undertaken should be with the entire approval and cooperation of the local public school officials;
3.   That so far as possible the fund should be used to help provide opportunities for effective training for rural life among the southern Negroes.

In keeping with this philosophy, funds awarded usually went for buildings, equipment, and teacher salaries (industrial).[36]

Three years later the Phelps-Stokes Fund, established and named for Mrs. Caroline Phelps-Stokes, also demonstrated special interest in black education–particularly industrial education. These funds were to be distributed and used regardless of race or nationality. The program of the Phelps-Stokes Fund called for the training of boys in the elementary grades in woodwork and in repairs about the school, farm, home, or shop. The girls' training was concentrated in the home and included practice in cooking and sewing. Both girls and boys were to be trained in simple carpentry, shoe mending, soldering, and furniture, window, and lock repair. Commensurate with other philanthropic organizations, the Phelps-Stokes trustees viewed industrial education as a means for preparing students for their life work and criticized blacks for their attempts to prepare students for college and not life. It is interesting to note that in 1912, the fund gave $12,500 to the University of Georgia for the appointment of "a Fellow of Sociology for the Study of the Negro."[37]

In 1910 Julius Rosenwald became interested in the improvement of conditions among blacks. He visited Tuskegee Institute and in 1912 became a member of the Tuskegee Board of Trustees. Beginning with small donations, Rosenwald gradually increased his contributions for the improvement of facilities for the education of southern blacks. He also provided funds to construct sixteen YMCA buildings and one YWCA for Negroes. However, it was not until 1917 that Rosenwald established a foundation for improving the quality of black education. With the use of about $40 million, the trustees of the Rosenwald Fund concentrated their efforts first on constructing rural school buildings, then on supporting high schools and colleges, and finally providing fellowships for Negroes and whites of unusual promise. Rosenwald also encouraged self-help among Negroes in northern cities by supplying matching funds (one-fourth in Chicago) if they raised the balance for building construction.[38]

There can be no doubt that the various philanthropic organizations facilitated black people's quest for an education, though in many respects it was enhanced in a negative way. The contributions of philanthropists, who overemphasized industrial training, generally improved education for both races in the South and stimulated self-help of individuals, institutions, and states—but often at the expense of the black liberal arts institutions which were forced to operate under financial strain.

Schools such as Fisk and Atlanta universities suffered financial losses because of their retention of the New England traditional educational system. W. E. B. DuBois was shocked when he returned to Fisk in 1908 to learn of a new Department of Applied Science. This urban institution was now teaching agriculture, animal husbandry, plant breeding, cooking, and sewing. The new curriculum had the support of, among others, the General Education Board, white citizens of Nashville, and the Slater Funds; so a number of black educators and institutions had to revise their curricula in a similar manner to attract funds.[39]

The South's educational problems were also intensified in the area of public education. Although white southerners would neither support nor attend racially integrated schools, the alternative which developed— segregated school systems—increased the financial burden of states unable to operate even a unitary system well. The dual system of education prevented the South from attaining quality education equal to the North's for the next seventy-five years.[40]

There were early signs that the system of Negro education was not working. The training instituted by the new England missionaries remained viable. Black communities, though closed and separate, demanded a literary education for their children in addition to an industrial education, which was emphasized in the rural schools. The needs of churches and businesses required more than industrial education. The aim of training blacks to accept their social caste in a democracy and to remain satisfied showed signs of failure.[41]

Special education did not prove to be an effective tool of economic adjustment for blacks as envisioned by Booker T. Washington. The whole ideology overlooked the current trends in the economic development of the country. Agriculture was rapidly declining as jobs opened up in manufacturing, commerce, trade, and administration. Industrial courses taught at Hampton and Tuskegee were almost obsolete from the beginning. Instead the schools were teaching hand laundering.[42]

Since the Negro lived in a closed society, the educational system was designed to develop technical and professional men and women to function within that society. Instead, what was created was a leadership class whose talents were not compatible to their society. They were technically and professionally trained beyond the needs of the black community and therefore unable to win acceptance in the larger community. These men and women harnessed their talents in an attempt to gain the equality promised them during the Reconstruction period.[43]

Special Education Challenged

The man who emerged to challenge Booker T. Washington and the whole ideological basis of industrial education and second class citizenship was William Edward Burghardt DuBois. Though he never achieved a national reputation as great as Washington's, DuBois established himself as a force to be dealt with. Rarely has history produced a situation in which the principals, Washington and DuBois, were so strikingly distinct. Washington began as a slave in Virginia, and DuBois was born a free Negro in Great Barrington, Massachusetts.

W. E. B. DuBois received an exceptional education for a Negro born during the nineteenth century. Between 1885 and 1894, DuBois attended Fisk University, Harvard College, and the University of Berlin. At Harvard, DuBois received his Doctor of Philosophy, and at the University of Berlin studied under Schmoller, Wagner, Sering, Weber, and von Treitschke. Under these scholars DuBois began to view "the race problem in America, the problem of the peoples of Africa and Asia, and the political development of Europe as one."[44]

When DuBois returned to the United States, he accepted the Chair of Classics at Wilberforce University with an annual salary of $80 and was appointed a professor of Latin and Greek. Just a few days after the Wilberforce offer, DuBois received a telegram from Booker T. Washington offering him a position at Tuskegee, which he turned down. In 1896 Harvard published DuBois's dissertation under the title *The Suppression of the African Slave Trade to the United States of America, 1638-1870*. This work by DuBois was the "first of the Harvard Historical Studies," published under the direction of the Department of History and Government; thus, W. E. B. DuBois began his life's work "not as an agitator nor as a carping critic of another's achievements, but as a painstaking investigator and a writer of remarkable lucidity and keenness."[45]

Through the initiative of Susan P. Wharton, a member of one of Philadelphia's oldest and most prominent Quaker families, DuBois was asked to study the problems of blacks in that city. DuBois arrived in Philadelphia in August 1896 and, except for two months, he remained there until January 1898. The finished product was the monumental sociological study, *The Philadelphia Negro*. The study received favorable reviews by the *Yale Review*, *The Annals of The American Academy of Political and Social Science*, *The Nation*, and *Outlook*.[46]

Following his studies of blacks in Philadelphia, DuBois began teaching at Atlanta University. While at Atlanta, DuBois inaugurated the Atlanta University Studies which covered virtually all phases of Negro life. He produced sixteen sociological monographs which were most remarkable when one considers the financial strain under which the university was operating between 1897 and 1914. Ballard has called DuBois's years at Atlanta University his "most productive scholarly period."[47]

In one of his essays, titled "The Study of the Negro Problems: (1898)," DuBois emphasized the need to analyze problems faced by blacks. In reviewing the history of blacks in the United States, DuBois cited two points: (1) the black masses had not reached a high level of culture and (2) there was an American "conviction" that black people should not be allowed to enter into the society "no matter what their condition might be."[48] On the education of blacks, DuBois stated:

> We hear much of higher Negro education, and yet all candid people know there does not exist today in the centre of Negro population a single first-class fully equipped institution devoted to the higher education of Negroes; not more than three Negro institutions in the South deserve the name of *college* at all; and yet what is a Negro college but a vast college settlement for the study of a particular set of peculiarly baffling problems? . . . Without doubt the first effective step toward the solving of the Negro question will be the endowment of a Negro college which is not merely a teaching body, but a centre of sociological research, in close connection and cooperation with Harvard, Columbia, Johns Hopkins and the University of Pennsylvania.[49]

DuBois obviously saw a greater future for black higher education institutions than merely the training of individuals. He viewed the research program at Atlanta University as the beginning of such a program.

While in Atlanta, DuBois published his famous *Souls of Black Folk* in 1903. The book was the compilation of several essays on blacks and contained a very critical analysis of Booker T. Washington. While attacking Washington's program, DuBois renewed the post-Civil War demands of political and social equality for blacks. DuBois began his criticism of Washington by stating that Washington's program "of industrial education, conciliation of the South, and submission and silence as to civil and political rights, was not wholly original." He went on to cite historical instances in which blacks strenuously worked to build industrial schools. Second, he stated that Washington accomplished the task of gaining the sympathy and cooperation of the South through his speech at the Atlanta Exposition in 1895, which DuBois labeled the "Atlanta Compromise." He called the compromise "the most notable thing in Mr. Washington's career."[50]

Washington's leadership was viewed as "a compromise between the South, the North, and the Negro." Washington's compromise was indeed unique. To DuBois, Washington appeared to ask blacks to relinquish political power and agitation for civil rights and higher education, and to emphasize industrial education and conciliation with the South. DuBois vividly pointed out the results of such a program: blacks had lost the vote, their legal status as citizens, and financial aid for black higher education institutions. He attributed these results to Washington's "propaganda."[51]

DuBois felt that Washington faced a "triple paradox" in his career. First, Washington was attempting to make blacks artisans, yet they would be unable to maintain even this position without the rights of the franchise. Second, while advocating thrift and self-respect, he simultaneously called for the submission of black people and their acceptance of an inferior class position in southern society. Finally, Washington advocated common-school and industrial training while debasing higher education. DuBois accurately pointed out that "neither the Negro common-schools, nor Tuskegee itself, could remain open a day were it not for teachers trained in Negro colleges, or trained by their graduates."[52]

DuBois went on to state that two classes of black Americans opposed Washington's position. The first class, which consisted of the descendants of Toussaint, Gabriel, Vesey, and Turner, represented an attitude of mutiny and vindication. The second class consisted of educated blacks, including the Grimké brothers, Kelly Miller, and J. W. E. Bowen. This group advocated the right to vote, social and political equality, and education according to ability. Though they acknowledged Washington's achievements, they felt that Washington's broad system of industrial education was not adequate. This group of protesters was surprised that ". . . a man of Mr. Washington's insight cannot see that no such educational system ever has rested or can rest on any other basis than that of the well-equipped college and university, and they insist that there is a demand for a few such institutions throughout the South to train the best of the Negro youth as teachers, professional men, and leaders."[53]

DuBois was not totally critical, and was willing to recognize Washington's accomplishments, most notably his attempts to appease members of the Louisiana and Alabama constitutional conventions and his opposition to the lynching of blacks. But Washington's demand that blacks strive for themselves was attacked because of past injustices, which now necessitated the aid and encouragement of the country's richer majority population if blacks were to make sustained progress. It is here that DuBois leveled his most severe criticism of Washington. He stated that Washington's doctrine ". . . tended to make the whites, North and South, shift the burden of the Negro problem to the Negro shoulders and stand aside as critical and rather pessimistic spectators." The burden, said DuBois, lay with the nation, and until that burden was dutifully carried, no one's hands would be cleansed. Thus, DuBois resolved to oppose Washington's program of submission and compromise. He concluded that as long as Washington preached his submissive program, it was the duty of all blacks to "unceasingly and firmly oppose" such a program.[54]

The same year that DuBois published *Souls of Black Folk,* he also published his educational philosophy under the title, "The Talented Tenth." In this paper, DuBois argued that blacks would be saved by their "exceptional men." Said DuBois, "The problem of education, then, among Negroes must first of all deal with the Talented Tenth; it is the problem of developing the Best of this race that they may guide the Mass away from the contamination and death of the Worst, in their own and other races."[55] The talented tenth, the vanguard to uplift the masses, was to be trained in the curriculum of higher education. DuBois wished to take the elite of black youth and educate them in institutions of higher education. DuBois viewed the university as ". . . a human invention for the transmission of knowledge and culture from generation to generation, through the training of quick minds and pure hearts, and for this work no other human invention will suffice, not even trade and industrial schools."[56]

One of the most important features of his paper on the education of blacks was the foundation that DuBois laid for the preservation and improvement of black colleges and universities. He briefly, but vividly, described several of the prominent black institutions, including Howard, Fisk, Shaw, Atlanta, Wilberforce, and Leland; and he noted that together they enrolled 750 black students. He also pointed out that the curriculum was one based upon liberal arts. Thus, by 1899 there were 2,079 male and 252 female black college graduates. Furthermore, 50% of those black students born in the North and 90% born in the South returned to, and remained in, the South to work towards improvement of the race.[57] But DuBois felt that the greatest contribution of the black colleges and universities was the training of black teachers.

The movement from slavery to freedom and the acquisition of a basic education in such a short period of time was a monumental accomplishment. The masses of black people were brought in contact with a new culture. Thus DuBois saw the role of teachers as vital in the transformation of black people to basic literacy. He felt that much of this was due to instilling in the teachers their responsibility to the race.[58]

The educational system that DuBois envisioned was to do more than train individuals in the trades. It was the black colleges that produced the teachers for the industrial schools. These institutions produced over ". . . 30,000 teachers and more." Said DuBois, "If Hampton, Tuskegee and the hundred other industrial schools proved in the future to be as successful as they deserve to be, then their success in training black artisans for the South will be due primarily to the white colleges of the North and the black colleges of the South, which trained the teachers who today conduct these institutions."[59]

The Tuskegee experiment, developed by Booker T. Washington, consisted of industrial training of blacks. However, in closing his paper on the "talented tenth," DuBois skillfully attacked Washington's basic philosophy. He pointed out that Tuskegee had instructors from Harvard, Oberlin, Atlanta, Fisk, and Smith, who had been instructed in the liberal arts of higher education and that Washington's wife, at one time, had been his classmate in the subject of Greek literature. Hence, his wife served as an example of the result and further need of higher education for blacks. Education was to "teach life." The "talented tenth" were to be the future leaders and no one else could accomplish the work. In the end, DuBois concluded, it is the black colleges which must educate the black race.[60]

In addition to DuBois's opposition, there grew a general aversion to Booker T. Washington's philosophy. It was at the end of President Theodore Roosevelt's term that this opposition began to form, with much of this resistance led by black intellectuals. Their beginnings were slow, but they grew to haunt Washington for the remainder of his life.

In March 1897 some eighteen black intellectuals organized the American Negro Academy in Washington, D.C. Its aim was to bring together the best minds of the black race in an attempt to stem the assault on black social, political, and educational rights. The first president, Bishop Alexander Crummell, advocated racial cooperation and self-help. However, a year before his death he accused white Americans of attempting to prevent the intellectual advancement of blacks. Black intellectuals were needed to aid in the education of the masses, and these ". . . scholar-leaders would give direction to the united effort against degradation." W. E. B. DuBois, who was one of the founders of the ANA, went even further than Crummell. In an essay titled "The Conservation of the Races," published 1897, DuBois targeted the problem of racial prejudice. He said it was nothing but friction between different groups of people even though these people could not possibly exist without some type of contact with each other. However, he did advocate the preservation and strengthening of the black race. Said DuBois, "As such, it is our duty to conserve our physical powers, our intellectual endowments, our spiritual ideals; as a race we must strive by race organization, by race solidarity, by race unity to the realization of that broader humanity which freely recognizes difference in men, but sternly depreciates inequality in their opportunities of development."[61]

As Booker T. Washington became more entrenched in his philosophy, the ANA scholars were forced into open opposition. They could not stand silent while Washington degraded the black race. The increased disfranchisement of blacks in the South and the cuts in state aid to public and higher education for blacks caused Archibald Grimké, DuBois, and W. S. Scarborough to support the greater ". . . relevance of political rights in determining the quality of education."[62]

Among the intellectuals in opposition to Washington was Professor John Hope of Atlanta University. Hope had been present during Washington's 1895 Atlanta Exposition speech and felt that Washington was wrong. With the aid of the American Baptist Home Mission, Hope in 1899 embarked upon a speaking tour in an attempt to spread the idea that blacks needed higher education, but he met with general apathy.[63]

Another black Harvard graduate, William Monroe Trotter, rose to become one of Washington's foremost critics. Working with Amherst graduate George Forbes. Trotter in November 1901 began publishing the *Boston Guardian*. From the beginning, the paper called for equal rights for blacks, and agreed with the position of black intellectuals. As the paper grew beyond the geographic scope of the Boston and New England area, Trotter increased his editorials against lynching, Jim Crow, and Booker T. Washington. Trotter continuously placed Washington in a compromising position. Since the central focus of his leadership required accommodation, he became a highly vulnerable target for Trotter's skillful snipings.[64]

Washington and Trotter confronted each other at what has become known as the "Boston Riot of 1903." When Washington appeared at the Boston Business League, he was met with stiff opposition. As he rose to speak, one of Trotter's associates, Granville Martin, rose to ask questions but was removed by the police. Then Trotter and Moses Newsome proceeded to shout questions at Washington. In the melee that resulted, Trotter and his associates were arrested by the police. Trotter thus became a martyr in DuBois's eyes.[65]

With the opposition to Washington increasing, Andrew Carnegie financed a secret meeting, called by Washington, at Carnegie Hall in New York in January 1904. There were some anti-Washington participants and a few white participants, including Oswald Garrison Villard and Carl Schurz, both of whom were founders of the National Association for the Advancement of Colored People.[66]

The Carnegie conference resulted in the establishment of the Committee of Twelve for the Advancement of the Interests of the Negro Race. During the conference, DuBois and Washington were supposed to have equal representation in addition to such neutrals as Kelly Miller. DuBois realized earlier that the committee was stacked against him, but attempted to work with it as it tried to negotiate problems with the Pullman Company. DuBois soon withdrew because he realized that Washington, as chairman, dictated the committee's activities. The rift between Washington and DuBois grew wider.[67]

On June 13, 1905, W. E. B. DuBois sent a letter to selected black leaders proposing a new organization. That letter was the seed which brought forth the Niagara Movement and ultimately the National Association for the Advancement of Colored People. In the letter, DuBois proposed that the organization present opposing views, organize for social and political rights, and ". . . establish and support proper origins of news and public opinion."[68]

Twenty-nine men from fourteen states were forced to meet on the Canadian side of Niagara Falls July 11-14, 1905, because of discriminatory practices of Americans. Of the twenty-nine, all but five were from the North. From this meeting came a "Declaration of Principles," which dealt with the problems of blacks in the areas of progress, suffrage, civil liberty, employment, education, law, public opinion, health, labor unions, church, armed services and others. With reference to education, the principles stated that high school education should not be the monopoly of one particular class or race in any section of the country.[69]

A second meeting was held at Harpers Ferry, West Virginia, August 16-19, 1906. This meeting place was used as a symbol of respect for John Brown. The document from the second meeting called for the education of black children. It demanded that the national government take a major role in terminating illiteracy in the South. DuBois declared, "We shall not be satisfied to take one jot or tittle less than our full manhood rights. We claim for ourselves every single right that belongs to a freeborn American, political, civil and social; and until we get these rights we will never cease to protest and assail the ears of America."[70]

Although the Niagara Movement never attained a membership of over four hundred, it did succeed in formalizing the split with Booker T. Washington. In addition, it succeeded in ousting Washington from control of the Afro-American Council.[71] However, it failed to achieve overall success against Washington.

In 1910 the National Association for the Advancement of Colored People was formed in New York. The interracial charter contained the names of several well-known progressive whites including Villard, Milholland, Lillian Wald, Jane Addams, John Haynes Holmes, Franz Boas, Moorfield Storey, and Clarence Darrow. W. E. B. DuBois was the only black among the chief officials of the organization. However, the organization did consist of a number of college-educated blacks. By 1914, the NAACP had 6,000 members in 50 branches, and *The Crisis,* edited by DuBois, had a circulation of 31,540.[72]

Clearly, throughout the process of the Niagara Movement and the founding of the NAACP, W. E. B. DuBois's leadership was a determining factor. His eloquence and style of leadership helped to enrich and develop an organization which eventually struck down the legal barriers to integrated education.

Throughout the first ten years of the twentieth century, DuBois confronted Washington on many issues. During the William Levi Bull Lectures, 1906-1907, in which both men participated, DuBois attacked the inadequacies of black schools, calling the situation "enforced ignorance." He stated that the black schools were worse than they were twenty years previously. The school terms were longer, the classes larger, but the salaries of teachers were lower.[73]

In a 1910 letter on industrial education to Edith R. Force of Oak Park, Illinois, DuBois raised the question of who was to benefit from the education of blacks, stating that if blacks were to be educated for their own benefit, then they should demand the highest education available.[74]

Though W. E. B. DuBois repudiated Washington's educational approach, he did not reject Washington's faith in the power of education. DuBois, believing in the powers of the intellectual and thus placing his faith in higher education, thought his fellow white Americans would not deny equal rights to an educated black elite.[75]

Both DuBois and Washington had an abiding faith in the power of education for black people. For example, in 1900 Washington wrote, "What the colored people are anxious about is that, with industrial education, they shall have thorough mental and religious training; and in this they are right." DuBois, when writing the resolutions for the Niagara Movement in 1906, stated that education was the "development of power and ideal." Washington believed that industrial education should teach students to meet the working conditions as they existed, and the skills the students learned were to enable them to earn a decent living. Finally, he believed that each student was to learn that there was dignity in labor.[76]

DuBois, however, saw many fallacies in this concept. He had been superbly trained in sociology. DuBois was partly aware that Washington's vision was doomed and futile from the very beginning. This is illustrated in DuBois's statement delivered to the Pan-African Conference in London in 1900 in which he said, "The problem of the twentieth century is the problem of the color-line, the question as to how far differences of race—which show themselves chiefly in the color of the skin and the texture of the hair—will hereafter be made the basis of denying to over half the world the right of sharing to their utmost ability the opportunities and principles of modern civilization."[77]

Because he understood American history and its emphasis upon the common man, Washington had an advantage over DuBois. DuBois's concept of the black masses being led by an educated elite put him at an extreme disadvantage. Washington's rise from slavery to a position of national leadership and acclaim provides special insight into his philosophy. He saw the common man rising, in accord with the American Creed, to greater heights on the basis of labor.[78] Inherent in the DuBois-Washington controversy was DuBois's fight against Washington's role in maintaining the racial status quo and his constant sniping at those blacks who called for an-all out struggle against the subjugation of the race. When Washington died in 1915, one of the major controversies in Afro-American history had ended. But by that time DuBois had clearly begun to rise as a prominent black leader.[79]

Washington was by no means the Uncle Tom his name later became associated with. Recent scholars (University of Maryland professor Louis Harlan, among others)[80] have shown how well Washington played the game and how he tried, in a number of instances, to manipulate behind the scenes in the interest of black people. But Washington was a spokesman for the old order. In the strictest sense he was not a leader, but a black man who vocalized attitudes that the white South, in agreement with the North, desired for the Negro in American society. Washington did not anticipate that even when the Negro had proved himself honest, thrifty, and industrious, he would remain suppressed, segregated, and disfranchised. While he viewed industrial education as the key to uplift the race, whites viewed it as the mechanism to keep blacks in second-class citizenship. Thus Washington was a tool used by southern whites to make blacks second-class citizens, and to provide a special system of education for them to make them not only feel inferior, but even more importantly, believe that they were inferior enough to accept this imposed second-class position in society.

Thus the years between 1890 and 1915 were crucial to black people: it was the period when white southerners, with northern acquiescence, relegated blacks to the lowest level in a caste system. Although W. E. B. DuBois and other progressive black leaders began to attack discrimination and violence against black people, they made little progress against the ramparts of racism. Even though major changes did not take place in race relations until after the *Brown* decision of 1954, the period between 1915 and 1954 was marked by a rising protest and a steady demand by black Americans for racial equality.

One of the most serious problems faced by blacks during this period was the establishment of separate but equal school systems which were separate but far from equal. Coupled with political, economic, and social deprivation, blacks had to contend with an educational system that was designed to thrust them into a second-class position. Progress, however, occurred in the area of black education over the next forty years in spite of the system.

CASTING DOWN THEIR BUCKETS
BLACK PEOPLE AND EDUCATION, 1915-1954

BLACKS DURING THE ERA OF THE FIRST WORLD WAR

With the birth of the NAACP there came the slow and painful process of attacking, primarily through the courts, the caste system established in the South, and to a lesser degree, throughout the nation. Prior to the United States' involvement in World War I, two significant cases were won before the Supreme Court by the NAACP. Under the leadership of Moorfield Storey, the organization's first president and a distinguished Boston lawyer, the NAACP brought about a major reversal in the efforts to keep blacks disfranchised. In 1915, the Supreme Court declared in *Guinn* and *Beal* v. *United States* that Oklahoma's "Grandfather Clause" violated the Fifteenth Amendment because it, in effect, disfranchised blacks. Again in *Buchanan* v. *Warley* (1917), the court ruled that a Louisville, Kentucky, ordinance providing for racial residential segregation was invalid because it violated the Fourteenth Amendment.[1] These early victories were significant, but the nation was not committed to racial equality and the South was left free to use a variety of subterfuges to get around the law and keep the black man in "his place."

A major phenomenon which occurred during the war era was the mass migration of blacks out of the rural South into urban areas of the South and North. The migrations serve as a testimony to black dissatisfaction with life in

the South and the extent to which blacks were exploited and denied opportunities for advancement. In addition to the legal barriers, blacks were forced
to live in constant fear. They no longer wanted to be exposed to mob violence
and lynchings of innocent people. Also, separate school facilities were
insufficient in number and inadequate to serve the communities. Black
students received a grossly inadequate share of equipment, supplies, and
structural space; and their teachers received salaries considerably lower than
that paid to whites. In addition to these conditions, many schools were opened
only three to five months out of the year.[2]

Another major cause of discontent was the way the sharecropping
system operated. Generally, white landowners supplied the land, equipment,
and necessary capital to their tenants in exchange for black labor and a
commensurate share of the crop. The lien system operated so that year after
year tenants found themselves deeper in debt. In addition, the black farmers
suffered doubly—from the destruction of their crops and from their indebted-
ness to landowners. From 1915 to 1917, the weather and boll weevil severely
damaged the cotton crop. Such devastation left both black and white farmers
without a means of support.[3]

Coupled with these elements pushing blacks out of the South was the
inducement, whether real or imagined, of the North. *The Chicago Defender*,
a widely read black weekly, continued a systematic campaign to attract blacks
to the North. A typical excerpt from one of its editorials read:

> Come to the north then, all you folks, both good and bad. If you don't
> behave yourselves up here, the jails will certainly make you wish you
> had. For the hard-working man there is plenty of work—if you really
> want it. The *Defender* says come.[4]

The *Defender* did not exaggerate increased employment opportunities, because the booming war business opened up positions for additional
employees. Blacks, as in other periods of American history, served as a
convenient reservoir of labor. Until the war generated the need for increased
production, blacks found employment in traditional fields of domestic and
personal service.[5]

With the beginning of the war, the high demand for war materials and
supplies resulted in a vast expansion of industry and an increased need for
labor. With the reduction in the volume of immigrants from Europe, due to
the quota imposed on the entry of aliens to the U.S., and the call to the military
of white industrial workers, utilization of the black migrant in industry

intensified. The enhanced opportunity also brought increased wages; wages offered blacks were double and even triple what they could earn in the South. Women who had earned as little as $2.50 per week, could earn $2.10 to $2.50 a day in northern industry. Men could earn between $2.50 and $3.75 a day, a considerable increase over what they received in the South.[6] Blacks were literally pushed out of the South by the agricultural demise and pulled North by increased economic opportunities.

Despite the call for black migration and the availability of employment, labor unions opposed black access to the trades. The reason for their opposition was that blacks were often used as strikebreakers, but since blacks found little or no opportunity for employment through labor unions, they were forced to become scab labor. Labor opposition to black workers confined blacks to the lower paying unskilled occupations.[7]

In April of 1917, when the United States declared war on Germany, black men were included in the call to the military service. Not only did blacks register when allowed to serve, but many answered the call by volunteering. The majority of black soldiers were assigned to noncombat units such as labor battalions and service regiments. Men who had received more than a high school education were appalled by their menial assignments and felt they should be trained as officers. To protest their exclusion, black soldiers established the Central Committee of Negro College Men. Through the efforts of this group, in conjunction with Joel E. Spingarn, a national officer of the NAACP, a training camp for black officers was established at Fort Des Moines, Iowa. Black soldiers displayed bravery in their job, in spite of the general attitude and resentment toward them.[8]

On their return to the United States in 1919, black forces received a tumultuous welcome as they marched past the cheering crowds of the urban North, but the black veterans' situation was not as promising as it seemed. Efforts to seek employment for the demobilized white soldiers had an adverse effect on the new black urbanite. The black veteran was faced with crowded cities, and virtually no jobs or opportunities to live in the country he so diligently fought for. In essence, the economic situation for blacks after the war was worse than it was before it.[9]

In fact, during the war years (1915-1918), 279 blacks were lynched. The Ku Klux Klan had been revived in 1915 in the South and also began to flourish in the North. Blacks defended their communities against mob violence from such secret organizations as the Klan. During 1919, a total of twenty-five riots occurred; so much blood was shed that James W. Johnson described it as the "Red Summer." The underlying causes of the riots were the white man's fear of employment competition, integration of his neighborhoods, and the progress of the black vote. White mob violence, by means of constant harassment, bombing, and murder made conditions in the black community deplorable Rioters acted without hindrance, due to inept and prejudiced local police. The state militia proved no better when called to bring the riots under control.[10]

THE STATUS OF BLACK EDUCATION BETWEEN THE WORLD WARS

Following World War I, it was apparent that Washington's industrial education had not prepared blacks for the realities of the twentieth century—labor unionism, factory systems, mass production and corporate enterprise. Not only did the general American education system lag behind the demands of an urbanized and industrialized society, but black education lagged behind that provided whites.[11]

The Negro college was the apex of the segregated system of education, and inherited students from inferior elementary and secondary schools. But in spite of the handicaps, the colleges proved to be of immense value to blacks and the nation. Whether viewed positively or negatively, Negro schools did help blacks to adjust to their social and economic situation.[12]

As has been shown, the burden of educating blacks fell on private individuals and organizations. The general lack of publicly supported high schools for blacks gave Negro colleges the added burden of providing for secondary education. Only as state-supported high schools were developed for blacks were colleges relieved of this responsibility, but state-supported black colleges were slow to offer college level work. Not one of the land-grant institutions developed under the Second Morrill Act offered college level work prior to 1916.[13]

Thus, when the United States Bureau of Education and the Phelps-Stokes Fund published their "Survey of Negro Education" in 1917, the survey basically described the state of Negro private education, especially in the South. The surveyors concluded:

No type of education is so eagerly sought by colored people as college education. Yet, no educational institutions for colored are so poorly equipped and so ineffectively organized and administered as the majority of those claiming to give college education.[14]

Fisk University in Nashville, Tennessee, and Howard University in the District of Columbia were the only schools acknowledged by the report to be of college and university proportions; yet even these schools had negligible endowments. Atlanta University, Morehouse College, Benedict College, and Lincoln University, among others, had as few as 10 percent of their total enrollment in college departments. These schools spent an average of only $100 per college level student. Although the report acknowledged the general deplorable situation of Negro education, there were exceptional students, teachers, and some good colleges.[15]

Since no black school offered the doctorate, it was incumbent upon predominantly white northern institutions to prepare blacks to assume their leadership role in the education of the race. Yet, prior to 1900, there were only seven blacks awarded the Ph.D. in this country. By 1920, the number had increased to twenty-one.[16] Thus, one can only conclude that white America expected blacks to educate themselves without the fundamental tools to do so. When blacks failed to measure up to normal standards, they were highly criticized.

The "Survey of Negro Education" further revealed that of the 61 northern colleges responding to a questionnaire, they enrolled a total of 390 black students of college caliber. Of these 390, 287 were in liberal arts; 70 in medical, dental, and pharmaceutical courses; 10 in law; 10 in theological schools; and 7 in veterinary medicine. The report estimated that there were approximately 500 black students in northern higher educational institutions. In addition, Howard University was the only black institution offering a full law course, which enrolled 106 students.[17]

The lack of qualified black professors forced most institutions to rely upon white instructors, as well as white trustees and administrators. This situation produced a problem for black institutions during the 1920s when black students became more aware of their racial heritage as the Harlem Renaissance began to bloom. Black students began to protest racial discrimination and predominantly white faculties. The students were often joined by black faculty members in their demand that blacks be placed in leadership positions on black campuses. In some instances, white college presidents and other administrative officers could not restrain their feelings of racial superiority and the contempt they held for black students. J. Stanley Durkee's quixotic behavior as president of Howard University and his evident contempt for such outstanding figures as Dean Kelly Miller were in part responsible for Durkee's resignation. He was replaced by Howard's first Negro president, Dr. Mordecai W. Johnson, elected by the Board of Trustees, September 1, 1926.[18]

Students also resented the way they were treated by college officials, who felt that it was their responsibility to serve not only in *loco parentis*, but, according to Herbert Aptheker, in place of stepparents. The white administrators maintained all of the racism prevalent in the nation at large. Black parents of the college students were unwilling to support the students in their protest. Education to them was so very important—that for their children to protest conditions, much less, to risk expulsion, was absolutely sacrilegious. Rather than have their children risk losing a college education, the parents were determined to see that their children remained in school, for parents knew too well the alternatives their children faced without a college education. It is well known that black colleges had to conform to a degree to the whims of southern racism, but whether they had to go to the extent some white and black officials did is open to question. When Tuskegee and Hampton announced new endowments totaling $5 million, DuBois urged their administrators to take advantage of the new opportunity to run the school for black students and not southern whites.[19]

As black students faced problems on black campuses, the problems they faced on white campuses markedly increased. All schools discriminated, but some were worse than others. The black student did not have to worry about the universities which blatantly discriminated; for these did not accept blacks. Less blatant forms of discrimination were practiced by such leading institutions as Princeton, Vassar, Harvard, Williams, University of Michigan, and Johns Hopkins. Acquiring an education in these schools was difficult at best. The generation of the twenties refused to remain silent. Even in the face of such obstacles to their education, the 1920s produced such leading figures as E. Franklin Frazier, William L. Hansberry, Ruth Anne Fisher, Arthur H. Fauset, Charles H. Houston, Horace M. Bond, and Jessie Fauset, and many talented others.[20]

It was the exception for a black to attend a predominantly white university. Black colleges and universities still had to shoulder the main responsibility for educating black people. Educators at black institutions took into serious consideration the criticism leveled at them by the 1917 Survey. Black institutions did wonders with funds provided by such foundations as the John F. Slater Fund, Julius Rosenwald Fund, The Peabody Education Fund and General Education Board. The Rosenwald Fund provided over $44 million for black education. Although much was spent in strengthening the foundation of Negro colleges, the fund generally emphasized the education of rural blacks by providing modern buildings.[21]

The John F. Slater Fund also channeled much of its financial aid into county training schools which continued to emphasize vocational education.

Between 1882 and 1932, Tuskegee and Hampton Institutes received a total of $604,500, while all the other black colleges and universities received a total of $1,216,845.76.[22] Even while black colleges were trying to shake the vocational philosophy of Washington and improve their academic programs, some foundations were reluctant to give up the idea that vocational education best suited the needs of black people.

Nevertheless, progress was made which was reflected in a subsequent survey in 1927. The survey was taken because of the failure of black college graduates to get into medical school, which illustrated to black educators the need for accreditation from a regional body. As part of the effort to obtain accreditation, the Federal Bureau of Education and the Phelps-Stokes Fund conducted a survey of seventy-nine colleges and issued their report in 1928. After that, the American Medical Association approved thirty-one colleges as being capable of providing pre-medical work. The survey also illustrated the great strides black colleges had made between 1916 and 1928. Most of those black institutions now concentrated primarily on college work and began to cut back and eliminate their elementary and secondary departments. Although the survey indicated great improvements had been made, it also pointed out the serious problems that remained: lack of financial support, library facilities, scientific equipment, and teachers and administrators. The table below illustrates this point.[23]

**Summary Facts from the Survey of
Negro Colleges for the Year 1926-27**

Description	*Number or Amount*
Number of College Students	12,000
Average per School	152
Volumes in Library	418,000
Average per School	5,200
Total Average Annual Expenditure on Library	$ 107,410
Average per School	$ 1,342
Total endowment	$20,713,796
Endowment of Hampton & Tuskegee Combined	$14,135,768
Endowment for Remaining 77 Schools	$ 6,577,928
Average Endowment for the 77 Schools	$ 85,426
Total Income	$ 8,516,291
Average per School	$ 108,000

The table shows there is no question of the fiscal inadequacy of the majority of these schools. Such great financial inadequacy dictated that other shortcomings would be evident.

Finally, in 1930, black educators succeeded in getting the Southern Association of Colleges and Secondary Schools to establish a system of inspections that could eventually lead to the placing of black colleges on an approved list of the association. The list meant only that these colleges met the association's minimum standards, but did not mean they were admitted as association members; the association excluded black colleges from membership. By 1936, sixteen four-year colleges had been classified as "Class A" and twenty-four as "Class B." The association maintained this system for black colleges until 1957 when fifteen colleges were admitted on an equal basis with white colleges.[24]

Excluded from membership in the Southern Association, black educators formed the Association of Colleges and Secondary Schools for Negroes in 1939 on the campus of Spelman College in Atlanta. Membership was offered to all approved Negro colleges regardless of their geographical location. This organization became a dynamic and powerful force in Negro education.[25]

The problem of Negro education remained, nevertheless, a general one in the 1930s. Public educational standards in the South were low, and for Negroes in the rural areas, even lower. The available elementary schools were impoverished and small. They lacked instructional equipment and were staffed with relatively unprepared, overworked teachers who were underpaid. Of those who finished these schools, few could find opportunity for secondary school education. Public undergraduate schools were limited and public graduate and professional opportunities nearly nonexistent. Xavier in New Orleans, Fisk, Howard, Atlanta, and Hampton were the only schools offering adequate graduate and professional education for blacks in the South. During the 1932-1933 school year, they held a combined enrollment of 300 students and graduated 76 students with the Masters of Arts degree.[26] Yet, no matter how inadequate the facilities, these colleges provided a much needed function.

By 1930 there were 19,000 students in black colleges. As they moved back into their communities as teachers, graduates from these colleges greatly aided in the reduction of illiteracy, which declined from 60 percent in 1895 to 25 percent in 1930. DuBois said in 1933 that the "American Negro problem is and must be the center of the Negro university." The small Negro college served the Negro students by providing individual attention and close contact with instructors. They served the adult community by teaching reading and writing in an attempt to correct the wretched system of public education. They were also extremely important in transmitting information on Negro life and history. Of seventy-one schools, forty-six offered seventy-one specific courses on the study of the Negro; fifty-two in Negro history. Even inside the classroom, through such direct and indirect activities as production of Negro music, plays, and Negro History Week, these colleges fostered knowledge of Negro life, tradition, and history.[27] Horace Mann Bond has aptly described these institutions:

> It [the Negro college] is, first, a college born of freedom. It is a college symbolizing man's highest conviction and belief in the equal endowment of all of the Sons of God with the highest mental qualities; and testifying to the right of enjoyment of every opportunity without distinction as to race or color.[28]

Prior to 1929, there were only fifty-one blacks who were awarded the doctorate, but one hundred nineteen were awarded between 1935 and 1939. The majority of these graduated from black schools. Harry Greene cites forty-eight from Howard University, eighteen from Lincoln University (Pennsylvania), sixteen from Fisk, sixteen from Morehouse, four from Hampton, and three from Tuskegee. They went on to receive their Ph.D.'s from some of the best schools in the nation: University of Chicago (25), Harvard University (25), and Yale University (10). These students proved that, given the opportunity, they could excel in the best graduate and professional schools. Yet, even these increased numbers of Ph.D.'s were not adequate to meet the needs of black colleges.[29]

In 1930, there were in 16 southern states and the District of Columbia, 9,552,815 blacks, with 18,550 in college, or one student per 515 black residents. The ratio of white college students in the same geographic area was 1 to 100. There should have been a total of 92,750 blacks in college to reach parity with the white population. But there were manifold problems—families could not afford to support children in college, and there were not enough secondary schools to prepare blacks for a college education.[30]

The separate but equal system of southern education had a major impact on the ability of blacks to enter those schools which were available to them. The problem began in the elementary and secondary schools. Although all provided for separate education, no state in the South provided equal education. The inequities were marked: salaries were lower for blacks, school terms shorter, value of property and equipment lower, and schools—especially high schools—were inaccessible to thousands. Blacks were denied what little cultural opportunities were available. For example, of the 7,000 public libraries in the United States, the South had only 802; of that number, only 121 rendered service to blacks.[31] These circumstances were hardly conducive to blacks acquiring quality education.

In addition to the widespread discriminatory treatment blacks received in their attempts to obtain an education, they were handicapped by the Great Depression of the 1930s. Southern blacks were faced with the added disadvantage of a higher unemployment rate than whites and discriminatory treatment by southern officials in charge of administering the New Deal relief program.

Over the years, southern agriculture became more and more characterized by tenant farmers. In 1880, 36.2% of all farmers were tenants. By 1930, the percentage had increased to 55.5% with blacks overly represented. Charles Johnson's study of tenants revealed that in 1933, they received an average of $105.43 a year per family; these families, theoretically, benefited from federal aid to farmers. Johnson described tenancy as a form of slave labor, whether black or white. Education and self-improvement were luxuries and had no place in the lives of tenants. Food, which basically consisted of salted fat pork, corn meal, and molasses, was not conducive to the development of a healthy body, much less a healthy mind.[32]

The situation for blacks was made even more deplorable by policies of the Agriculture Adjustment Administration. Owners of cotton land contracted with the Secretary of Agriculture to plow up between 25 and 50 percent of their acreage and in return received a rental payment of approximately $11.00 per acre. Cotton producers received double their income of the previous year. The tenants were the ones who suffered. They were to receive a share of the government's payment, but in reality, they received little or nothing. Again, tenants could not take advantage of low credit interest rates of 4½ to 6½ percent unless landowners waived their liens on the crops. Usually the landowners received the low interest loans and gave their tenants credit at the rate of 20 to 30 percent.[33] Prior to the depression the system operated to the detriment of blacks, but during the depression the plight of blacks deteriorated further.

Not only did blacks in the rural areas suffer, but the situation of urban blacks was particularly insecure. In 1935, in the urban South, one out of ten white families received public assistance compared with one-fourth of all black families. The substantially greater amount of public aid provided to blacks in the North encouraged a number to migrate to northern urban areas. With the active cooperation of the NAACP and others, blacks corrected many of the discriminatory practices of various federal programs. Through the advice of President Franklin D. Roosevelt's "black cabinet" and the interest of Mrs. Roosevelt, blacks became more actively involved in federal programs as the New Deal moved from providing doles to providing jobs. Because blacks were the hardest hit by the depression—last hired, first fired—they generally benefited from federal efforts in spite of discrimination.[34]

BLACKS, WORLD WAR II, AND THE POSTWAR YEARS

World War II was of extreme importance to the recovery of not only the United States' but the Western World's economy. The New Deal had not been able to achieve full utilization of the existing productive capacity and consequently, unemployment remained a critical problem. The need to build up the armed forces was a pressing issue. The number of officers and soldiers was below the level of World War I, and black soldiers in the army had diminished significantly. By 1940, the United States Army consisted of two hundred thirty thousand enlisted men and officers, but there were less than five thousand Negroes.[35]

The building of United States defense served as a catalyst for economic recovery. The utilization of idle industrial plants, either directly in defense or as an effect of war-induced activity, meant full employment of the labor force and increased opportunities for blacks. However, while preparation for war and finally involvement in World War II created economic stability, correspondingly a political and social contradiction began to surface around the treatment of black people within industry as well as the armed forces. Hitler's ideology of racial hegemony was considered revolting by most whites. Black people concurred but took issue with the practice of segregation and discrimination in the United States, which they correctly understood as rooted in the same principle as Nazism, viz., racism. A number of black people believed that the menace of racism should be fought tenaciously, yet they found racist restrictions in the practice of selective service boards contrary to the notion of defeating fascism and white supremacy.

Blacks did not fail to protest United States military discriminatory policies. In September 1940, a group of Negro leaders—A. Philip Randolph, Walter White, and others—submitted a seven-point program to assure Negro participation in the defense programs. They urged, among other things,

. . . that all available reserve officers be used to train recruits; that Negro recruits be given the same training as whites; that existing units in the army accept officers and men on the basis of ability and not race; that specialized personnel, such as physicians, dentists, and nurses be integrated; that responsible Negroes be appointed to draft boards; that discrimination be abolished in the Navy and Air Forces; and that competent Negroes be appointed as civilian assistants to the Secretaries of War and Navy.[36]

The government's attempt to discourage discrimination proved unsuccessful, amounting to mere gestures, because no enforcement powers were provided. One example was the Negro Employment and Training Branch of the Office of Production Management's Labor Division. The War Department announced that blacks would be admitted to the army in numbers proportionate to their amount of the total population and would be organized into segregated units. The appointment of William H. Hastie, Dean of Howard University Law School, as Civilian Aide on Negro Affairs to the Secretary of War, and Major Campbell Johnson as Executive Assistant to the Director of Selective Service, did little to subdue protests of continued discriminatory practices. Even the promotion of Colonel Benjamin O. Davis, to become the first black brigadier general, failed to effect a change in existing policies. Blacks were not hired in the defense industries because it was said that they did not possess the necessary skills; yet their education and training had been designed to assure that they would not gain the necessary skills to compete with whites. As they did during World War I, blacks secured jobs that were left by whites who went to war or obtained better paying positions.[37]

Appalled by job discrimination, blacks picketed defense industries and marched in protest. A. Philip Randolph, President of the Brotherhood of Sleeping Car Porters, threatened to organize a national "Negro March on Washington," to take place on July 1, 1941. In the interim, President Roosevelt attempted to call the march off, but Randolph emphasized that only an executive order prohibiting employment bias in defense industries could stop him. Subsequently, on June 25, 1941, Roosevelt issued Executive Order 8802, which essentially stated the government's position of nondiscrimination in employment.[38]

The order commanded all departments of the federal government and the vocational training program to make their services available to more blacks, and for defense contracts to cease discriminatory hiring practices and to delete clauses providing such practices from their contracts. The pertinent part of the order stated:

. . . [t]here shall be no discrimination in the employment of workers in defense industries or Government because of race, creed, color or national origin. . . . And it is the duty of employers and of labor organizations . . . to provide for the full and equitable participation of all workers in defense industries, without discrimination because of race, creed, color or national origin. . . .[39]

In addition, the order established a Committee on Fair Employment Practices as its functioning arm to address violations of the order through public hearings. As a result blacks received jobs in the various war industries, especially in aircraft plants such as Lockheed, thereby acquiring new skills and higher salaries.[40]

By 1942, there were over fifty-eight thousand black people enrolled in such employment training programs as the National Youth Administration and the Works Progress Administration, which trained civilian mechanics. Students in black colleges were enrolled in the engineering, science, and management war training programs, under the auspices of the United States Office of Education. By the end of the war blacks were working in most major industries and serving in the Red Cross, Nurses Aides, and the Motor Corps.[41]

Black soldiers were more active than they were in the first war. Blacks served in the infantry, coast and field artillery, cavalry, tank battalions, transportation units, and signal, engineer, and medical corps. They were registered in the Women's Army Corps and later in pilot squadrons. Reserve Officers Training Corps was established at the end of World War I at Howard University and Wilberforce University. During the second war, Civilian Pilot Training units were established at West Virginia State College, Hampton Institute, North Carolina Agricultural and Technical State University, Prairie View College, and Tuskegee Institute. Entry into the war shifted so many black males from the college campus to the battlefield that one college president for Negro men thought that the war would mean the end of his and other colleges in similar situations. But the United Negro College Fund, organized in October 1943, sustained black colleges with financial assistance in their time of need.[42]

Nevertheless, the effect of World War II placed a considerable burden on black schools. A study performed by the Federal Security Agency of the U.S. Office of Education pointed out the decline of educational institutions during the war:

Their men students have been drafted; their faculties have been "raided"; and their recruits from teacher education institutions have been greatly decreased. The job of teaching, particularly in many public schools, in some instances has been turned to untrained youth, which has affected the discipline of schools. In addition, finances have been depleted and the general equipment and state of repair of buildings frequently leave much to be desired.[43]

Schools scarcely had recovered from the depression when construction on college campuses stopped due to the shortage of materials. The postwar boom brought the largest income the schools had ever known, only to be followed by severe inflation.[44] This created problems not only for the black students, but also for their institutions.

Colleges and students both benefited from either the Veterans Readjustment Program or the G.I. Bill of Rights. This comprehensive legislation contained numerous rights and benefits available to veterans and their dependents, among them, provisions for training and education at any institution approved by the Veterans Administration. The length of training was not to exceed the length of time the veteran spent in active service after September 1, 1940, and before the end of the Korean War, to a maximum of four years. Expenses paid included tuition, laboratory and library payments, and cost of books and supplies. While in school the veteran and his dependents, if any, were allotted a monthly living allowance.[45]

The G.I. bill had a direct effect on black education. Between 1919 and 1939 the male to female ratio in private black colleges was approximately equal. However, in 1949 enrollment was about 56 percent male. The impact of the G.I. bill can also be ascertained when 1939-1940 (prewar year) statistics are contrasted with the 1949-1950 statistics showing over an 85 percent increase in total enrollment.[46] These figures explicitly show how government financial aid can have an immediate and progressive impact by availing black people increased opportunities.

The postwar years were marked by an ever-growing black militancy. World events, together with black demands, forced the federal government, especially the executive branch, to respond favorably to the plight of blacks. President Truman's Executive Order 9808, issued on December 5, 1946, created a Presidential Committee on Civil Rights. The committee issued a report, *To Secure These Rights,* in which it condemned racial segregation and the general denial of blacks' civil rights. Though integration had begun in the armed forces during World War II, Truman's Executive Order 9981 was the first step toward eliminating segregation, albeit not discrimination in the armed services.[47]

World War II created many changes, one of which was integration of the armed forces. The cold war stimulated the need for additional changes as the United States was propelled into the leadership position of the western world. The United States could no longer afford to project a world-wide image of a racist country which discriminated against its minorities. This was particularly true as African and other colonized countries began to demand their independence. In the ideological struggle with communist countries, the United States was at a disadvantage. The paradox of the United States' position vis-à-vis minorities was readily apparent as the United States claimed to be the leaders of the "free" world.

The end of World War II and the beginning of the cold war seemed to have brought about a new high in black awareness. Although blacks had consistently protested against racial discrimination, the postwar years created a sense of urgency. The G.I. bill provided black men with the opportunity to extend their education, but opportunities were still limited by the barriers of segregation.

Although blacks themselves, with the aid of sympathetic whites, made substantial progress in the field of education, many realized that it was not enough. The private universities and white northern schools just were not producing enough trained men and women to meet the demands. Of the 117 Negro institutions of higher education in the United States, only 36 were publicly supported. Although 7 states provided scholarships for out-of-state graduate and professional study, those states with the largest percentages of blacks (29 to 50 percent) made no provisions for graduate work.[48] These facts brought many—especially the NAACP—to conclude that the doctrine of separate but equal, as a barrier to black educational opportunity, had to go.

A major test case came in 1935, although the case was not appealed to the Supreme Court. The NAACP began its attack in a border state where resistance to integrated higher education was believed to be not as great as in the deep South. Donald Murray applied to the University of Maryland's Law School, but was denied admission by its registrar. He filed a *mandamus* suit against the university on the grounds that his constitutional rights as a citizen of Maryland had been violated although his educational qualifications were sufficient. Since Maryland had no law school for blacks, and its out-of-state tuition amounted to only $200, the Maryland Circuit Court of Appeals directed the officers and regents of the university to admit him.[49]

A similar suit was filed in Missouri which reached the Supreme Court in *Missouri et rel. Gaines* v. *Canada* (1938). After Lloyd Gaines graduated from Lincoln University, Missouri, with the degree of Bachelor of Arts, he sought admission to the University of Missouri Law School. Since the state barred Negroes from attending its white institutions, the state provided tuition grants for blacks seeking education in areas not offered at Lincoln. Gaines rejected the idea of having to travel outside of his state to receive an education in law. The Supreme Court decided that ". . . here, petitioner's right was a personal one. It was as an individual that he was entitled to the equal protection of the laws, and the State was bound to furnish him within its borders facilities for legal education substantially equal to those which the State there afforded for persons of the white race, whether or not other Negroes sought the same opportunity." Southern states were confronted with either having to provide black public colleges with new facilities or having to admit black students to the white state-supported universities. Unfortunately, Gaines never entered the university; instead, he mysteriously disappeared. Missouri opened a separate law school for Negroes that, for a while, allowed the state to escape the issue of integrated higher education.[50]

The first real victory in the NAACP's campaign against segregated facilities came in 1948 in *Sipuel v. Board of Regents of the University of Oklahoma*. The case involved the state's refusal to admit a qualified black student to the state law school. The court was unanimous in its decision that as long as Oklahoma provided legal education for its white students, the petitioner was entitled to study law in a state institution. The court ruled that denial of the applicant's admission violated the equal protection clause of the Fourteenth Amendment.[51] The NAACP's deliberate assault on segregated higher education was beginning to produce results.

It became more and more evident that segregation in higher education was practically impossible with the recent decisions of the court. In an attempt to provide legal education for black citizens of Texas, the state established a Negro law school as an adjunct of the University of Texas. Marion Sweatt refused to attend the Negro school and applied to the white law school. He was denied admission. The suit appeared before the Supreme Court in *Sweatt v. Painter* in 1950. Chief Justice Vinson, speaking for a unanimous Court, held that the Negro law school established by the state did not provide in fact a truly equal education in law. The Chief Justice pointed out the inequality between the two schools in such things as the library, faculty, and prestige of the schools. He concluded that Sweatt's exclusion from the school violated the equal protection clause of the Fourteenth Amendment.[52] Although no attack was made on the separate but equal doctrine as such, it was clear from the decision that the Court's arguments could be used by blacks to gain admission into any graduate or professional school in the South.

Decided the same day as the Sweatt Case was the case of *McLaurin* v. *Oklahoma State Regents*. After a legal battle, George McLaurin had forced the state of Oklahoma to admit him to the graduate school of the state university. Once admitted, however, the school authorities segregated him in class in a section marked "reserved for colored." He was required to eat at a special reserved table in the dining hall and to use a special desk in the library. The court ruled that segregation of this sort within the school was unconstitutional. Chief Justice Vinson held that these restrictions impaired McLaurin's ability to effectively learn his profession and handicapped him in his pursuit of graduate instruction. They also deprived him of his "personal and present" right to an equal education. The court held that once admitted, McLaurin was entitled to the same treatment by the state as students of other races.[53]

Although these cases did not overturn the doctrine of separate but equal, they did prepare the NAACP's case for a direct assault on Jim Crowism in education. The NAACP did not limit its attack to separate education. There was a concerted campaign to invalidate the separate but equal doctrine in other areas of public interest. Attacks were made on such things as segregated public libraries, tax-supported hospitals, and public carriers.[54]

After nearly sixty years of enforced racial segregation and inequality, the NAACP, in conjunction with other interested organizations and individuals, was pressing hard to get the country to admit the inconsistency of the *Plessy* doctrine with equality as guaranteed by the Constitution. The test case came in the *Brown* decision in 1954. The unfortunate thing was that it was so long in coming. Generations of black people had suffered immeasurable, irrevocable damage. The history of black people from 1915 to 1954, especially in relation to education, is one in which the country consistently denied blacks opportunities for advancement. Only through their own ingenuity were they able to take advantage of the little resources made available. In 1954, the Supreme Court reaffirmed the nation's commitment to black people and the Fourteenth Amendment. But the question remained: was that enough? Could declaring segregation and discrimination illegal compensate a whole race for generations of inequality? The current plight of black people suggests that, just as the nation deliberately and consistently discriminated against blacks and denied them equal opportunities, especially in the areas of education, it is now time to take the necessary affirmative action to overcome the institutionalization of race prejudice and discrimination.

V.

THE CONTEMPORARY PLIGHT OF BLACK PEOPLE IN AMERICA, 1954 TO THE PRESENT

THE BROWN DECISION OF 1954 AND SCHOOL LITIGATION

The cases cited in the previous chapter established the practical impossibility of separate but equal schools. The NAACP was now prepared to begin its decisive campaign to gain equal educational opportunities for black people. Unlike the earlier phase of its attack, the NAACP's aim was to destroy once and for all the legal basis for segregation as public school policy. Under the guidance of its legal defense department, the NAACP attempted to get the Supreme Court "to rule on the legality of segregation itself and to consider as a basis for its judgment nonlegal materials that would possibly assess the inequalities inherent in segregation more realistically than would conventional legal evidence."[1]

The assault came when the Supreme Court agreed to consolidate the cases of *Brown* v. *Board of Education of Topeka,* the District of Columbia case of *Bolling* v. *Sharpe,* the Delaware case of *Gebhart* v. *Belton,* the South Carolina case of *Briggs* v. *Elliott,* and the Virginia case of *Davis* v. *County School Board of Prince Edward County.* The federal district court had ruled against Brown in 1951, considering itself bound by the *Plessy* decision. The district court found that the black and white schools were substantially equal and that in their maintenance and operation, there was no "willful, intentional, or substantial discrimination.'' Thus this case emphasized the inherent inequality in the segregated schools under attack.[2]

It was not difficult for the NAACP to illustrate the damage done by segregation to black people as individuals and as a group. The NAACP, had a long history of waging legal battles in its effort to improve the crowded conditions of black communities and the resultant social problems. They were now prepared to make their case that "segregation in and of itself was damaging to Negro children."[3]

The Court decided unanimously in all five cases that school segregation violated the constitution. Chief Justice Earl Warren gave the Court's opinion which largely avoided the legal and historical complexities of the case. Regardless of what the authors of the Fourteenth Amendment, had intended Warren thought it obvious, in view of conditions in the twentieth century, that school segregation imposed an inferior status on the Negro. Segregation produced a feeling of inferiority in Negro children; it damaged their minds and hearts to such a degree that it might not be undone. The Court concluded that school segregation violated the equal protection clause of the Fourteenth Amendment. Although the *Brown* decision implied that the *Plessy* decision had been overruled, the Court officially declared segregation unconstitutional in a case growing out of the Montgomery bus boycott. In *Gayle* v. *Browder* (1956), the Supreme Court confirmed a district court's decision that bus segregation was unconstitutional.[4]

In the *Brown* case, the Court did not issue an enforcement order, but instead asked for re-arguments on the ways in which the decision should be implemented. In May 1955, the Court issued its enforcement order. The Court returned the cases to the lower courts instructing them to work out the obstacles and to admit, "with all deliberate speed," the parties involved to public schools on a racially nondiscriminatory basis. Although the Court found that the black children had a categorical right under the Fourteenth Amendment to attend nonsegregated schools, the Court did not instantly provide them with this right. Instead, the Court chose to take into consideration the social revolution involved in the case when it ordered desegregation; so after admitting unequivocally that segregation in public schools deprived black children of the equal protection of the laws, the court ruled in favor of a deferred and gradual extension of the rights of black children. One author suggests that there was no constitutional justification for such a ruling. After the Court ruled in favor of the plaintiffs, not one single black child involved in the case from Clarendon County, South Carolina and Prince Edward County, Virginia ever attended integrated schools.[5]

The decision played into the hands of bitter southerners, who immediately began a protracted campaign to nullify the decision. The long-dead idea of "interposition" was resurrected. Seven southern states adopted interposition resolutions against the *Brown* decision in an attempt to void its impact in each state. Although the whole doctrine was constitutionally absurd, the states acted anyway and constructed their resistance movement on the basis that they could prevent the federal government from carrying out federal policy within state borders.[6]

In an attempt at massive resistance, southern states initiated a number of measures designed to circumvent the law of the land: southerners passed laws which permitted local school officials to transfer students to maintain segregation; they provided tuition grants so white children could be withdrawn from public schools; they threatened the withdrawal of state funds if schools were integrated; and they provided for the closing of schools as a last resort.[7]

The NAACP responded with a massive program of litigation in the federal courts in an attempt to force early compliance with the *Brown* decision. As the NAACP attempted to force government officials in the South to abide by the law, frustrated whites resorted to violence in a last ditch effort to keep blacks from receiving quality education.[8]

One well-known instance of interposition occurred in Little Rock, Arkansas when Governor Orval Faubus tried to prevent black children from entering the white high school by using the Arkansas National Guard. The Governor was forced to withdraw the National Guard, but the tone had already been set. The next day, as black children attempted to enter the school, they were prevented from doing so by an ugly mob of whites. It was then that President Eisenhower sent federal troops to Little Rock to uphold the decision. The use of federal power by President Eisenhower was decisive in determining the relationship between federal and state government and constitutional authority. The order to put the Arkansas National Guard under federal service to protect the black students was a major blow to the segregationist smoke screen of states rights.[9]

Because of the turmoil within the school system, the Board of Education obtained a two-and-one-half year stay against integration. The stay was reversed by the United States Court of Appeals. In *Cooper* v. *Aaron* (1958) the Supreme Court confirmed the reversal and took the opportunity to admonish the state for its futile attempt to frustrate federal authority. The Court said that the constitutional rights of children regardless of race "can neither be nullified openly and directly by state legislators or state executive officials nor nullified indirectly by them by evasive schemes for segregation."[10]

The volume of case law in the area of school desegregation is evidence of how school authorities had virtually ignored the *Brown* mandates. In holding unconstitutional the system of state aid to white children attending all-white private schools, the Supreme Court stated in *Griffin* v. *County School Board of Prince Edward County, Virginia* (1964),[11] "The time for more deliberate speed has run out." Still later in *Green* v. *County School Board of New Kent County, Virginia* (1968),[12] the court found desegregation policies insufficient when the freedom of choice plan alone was viewed as not an end in itself to remedy dual systems. In stating its judgment the Court concluded that "The burden on a school board today is to come forward with a plan that promises realistically to work, and promises realistically to work now."

In spite of these harsh words, state and local school authorities continued to neglect their duty to desegregate. In 1971, the Court found very much alive the same issues in *Swann* v. *Charlotte–Mecklenburg Board of Education*[13] concomitant with the issue of busing. Among the problems confronting the Court were the limitations, if any, on the use of busing to correct state enforced segregation. In view of the *Brown* decision, which required the elimination of dual educational facilities, the Supreme Court then upheld a lower court's ruling that busing of school children was a legitimate tool of the state in fulfilling its consitutional obligation to desegregate public education. The Court stated that "Desegregation plans cannot be limited to the walk-in school."[14] However, time and distance of travel must be so as to assure it will not impose on the health or the process of education of the children being transported. Such a consideration has essentially opened a mechanism to reject busing to achieve quality education. Federal district courts have wide remedial powers subject to their discretionary judgment. In a companion case, *North Carolina Board of Education* v. *Swann,*[15] the Court held invalid a state statute prohibiting busing to achieve racial balance. The Court emphasized: "Just as the race of students must be considered in determining whether a constitutional violation has occurred, so also must race be considered in formulating a remedy."[16]

The pattern of future school construction and abandonment was the subject in a companion case, *Davis* v. *Board of School Commissioners* (1971),[17] in which the Court emphasized that school authorities must assure that future proposals for constructing or abandoning schools will not serve to create dual schools. The Court evaded per se the de facto-de jure nomenclature, but did infer the presence of de facto segregated schools and stated that the existence of such required authorities "to satisfy the Court that their racial composition is not the result of present or past discriminatory action on their part."[18]

Decisions beginning with *Green* and culminating in *Swann* apply, for the most part, to southern school boards which had established by law dual school systems. Yet these decisions are relevant to the northern school problem of de facto segregation. Referring to the *Green* and *Swann* decisions, Frank Goodman, professor of Law, University of California, Berkeley, says:

> First, they cast a retrospective light on the meaning of Brown and, more especially, upon the status of the 'finding' that segregation does psychological and educational harm to Negro children. The *Green* and *Swann* cases . . . suggest a more central role for Brown's empirical finding. In imposing an affirmative duty to end what might be called 'post-de jure' segregation—continued racial imbalance in schools formerly segregated by law—these cases presuppose that de jure segregation has ill effects that continue even when legislative racial classification is removed.[19]

Thereafter, the Court was confronted with intentionally imposed segregative policies supported by state action. This type of segregation, commonly referred to as de facto segregation, was the subject in *Keys* v. *School District No. 1, Denver, Colorado* (1973).[20] Here, parents of Denver school children brought suit alleging the school board, by "manifestation of student attendance zones, school site selection and a neighborhood school policy, created and maintained racially or ethnically (or both racially and ethnically) segregated schools throughout the school district . . ."[21] The majority opinion emphasized that the burden on the plaintiffs is to prove that segregated schools exist in the school district, in spite of the authorization of *Brown I,* imposing an affirmative duty on the states to eliminate a dual system. The Court found that the plaintiffs had successfully established a prima facie case of segregative intent, and thereby granted them a decree directing the school authorities to desegregate the entire district.

Mr. Justice Douglas filed a separate opinion projecting the view that there is no real difference in de jure and de facto segregation in cases of this nature. He stated the following: "There is no constitutional difference between de jure and de facto segregation, for each is the product of state actions or policies. If a 'neighborhood' or 'geographical' unit has been created along racial lines by reason of the play of restrictive covenants . . . there is state action in the constitutional sense because the force of law is placed behind those covenants."[22]

In *Milliken* v. *Bradley* (1974),[23] the Supreme Court refused to impose a statewide multi-district desegregation remedy because of de jure segregation in a single district. The Court's decision was based on the absence of findings that the other districts had followed a policy which led to segregation across district boundaries.

In *Floyd* v. *Trice* (1974),[24] the U. S. Court of Appeals for the circuit encompassing Texarkana, Arkansas, granted injunctive and declaratory relief to black students in their suit against the Texarkana Superintendent of Schools. The students alleged that present discriminatory policies in the schools" . . . will have a further deleterious effect on the students after they graduate and move into the adult world." The court went further to state that such policies ". . . perpetuate the kind of school system and the resulting lack of future opportunity dealt with by the Supreme Court in *Brown I.*"[25]

In a comprehensive class action suit against the Secretary of the Department of Health, Education and Welfare, emphasis moved from access to education to that of equality. The suit known as *Adams* v. *Richardson* (1973),[26] was aimed at both public elementary and secondary schools as well as higher educational institutions. Plaintiffs sought a federal district court to compel HEW to cease providing federal funds to those institutions that still practiced racial discrimination in derogation of Title VI of the Civil Rights Act of 1964.

Attorneys for the plaintiffs, the NAACP Legal Defense Fund, took the position that if pressure was not exerted by the federal government, the states would neither desegregate black colleges nor strengthen them. Their view was to increase opportunities for blacks in higher education. But the National Association for Equal Opportunity in Higher Education, an organization of black college presidents, asserted in an amicus curiae brief that any attempt to change the identity of black colleges would result in closing, merging or absorption, of these institutions. The brief further stated:

> The Black Institutions of Higher Education have served and continue to serve as the bridge between a crippling and debilitating elementary and secondary educational system to which *Brown* itself was directed . . . Eighteen years after Brown, with a general consensus that this feeder system has not been improved and maybe has lost ground, the assimilation of the Black Institutions of Higher Learning would be to remove the wooden beam in order to replace it with a steel or cement support before the new beam is in place, leaving the structure unsupported at all.[27]

At the same time *Adams* was under consideration, a Georgia federal

district court decided *Hunnicutt* v. *Burge* (1973).[28] The court held that
all-black Fort Valley State College was not only inherently unequal but also
factually unequal and thus its program was designed to serve and attract only
black students. The court further ordered the board to ". . . revise and change
the educational program of Fort Valley State College so as to eliminate this
program designed for black students." The court went on to conclude the
following:

> All that is said therein is not to be construed by anyone as a finding by
> this court or an opinion of this court that the present state of this college
> results from the intentional, evil designs of anyone—it obviously flows
> from the benign neglect of those who do not wish to disturb or change an
> old but outmoded institution. Nevertheless, change we must![29]

This case set a precedent for what could possibly be a series of other cases
designed to end the black identity of black higher educational institutions.

Black institutions have not been counterracist. They have always sought
justice and racial equality for those who have suffered inequities because of
their black skins. Civil rights attorney Herbert O. Reid, Sr., in an article
entitled "Twenty Year Assessment of School Desegregation," presented at
the Topeka Education Conference in November 1974, stated the significance
of black colleges:

> The doors of Black institutions without exception have, from the begin-
> ning of their existence, been open to all races, sex, colors, creeds, and
> they have always collectively offered employment and other incidental
> privileges to all who passed through their doors, except where State law
> prohibited the same. They have been menders, and healers for wounded
> minds and restless souls. They have produced sterling talent which has
> benefited this Republic beyond measure of calculation—not only in
> material contribution, but intellectual, cultural, moral and spiritual of-
> ferings. In a number of instances, Black institutions have been more
> profoundly representative of the American ethic than the larger, more
> affluent, schools of Higher Education in this country. Indeed, they have
> been and remain today a domestic "Marshall Plan" committed to a
> public offering of education attainment in fee simple absolute, rather
> than an illusory expectancy of educational opportunity.[30]

The issue of minority preferential admission programs was presented to the Supreme Court in *DeFunis* v. *Odegaard* (1974).[31] However, the Court dismissed the case as moot, for DeFunis was subsequently admitted to the University of Washington School of Law and was about to graduate, thereby leaving no decree on the matter. The plaintiff, a white male who had been denied admission to the University of Washington Law School, sought a Court injunction to compel his admission, alleging the school's policy extending preferential treatment to minority students with lower evaluation ratings invidiously discriminated against him because of his race, and such action violated the equal protection clause of the Fourteenth Amendment. The Court rendered a per curiam opinion expressing the inadequacy of the merits because it did not satisfy constitutional case or controversy requirements. However, Mr. Justice Douglas dissented in a minority opinion and expressed the position that the case should be remanded to ascertain whether DeFunis in fact had been invidiously discriminated against because of his race.

Of the many amicus curiae briefs submitted in the *DeFunis* case, the one submitted by the National Conference of Black Lawyers asserted the following in favor of the university's preferential treatment policy: "Respondents' minority admissions plan is not rendered invalid because it alters expectations rooted in societal patterns that perpetuate racial inequality."[32] Such policies are directed to cure the badges and incidents of post-slavery which have victimized black educational attainment.

By virtue of the Court's holding in *Green*, ". . . a strong argument could be made for the proposition that integration is a compelling governmental interest. Thus, preferential minority admission programs should not be characterized as reverse discrimination, but as the reversal of discrimination."[33] The government has a compelling interest or, even more so, an obligation to counter future discriminatory acts that clearly violate the constitutional and legislative guarantees mandating equality in education.

It is evident from a cursory review of court cases since *Brown* that the battle has yet to be won. The *Brown* decision gave black children the constitutional right to an equal education, but the Supreme Court refused to make that right present and immediate because of the alleged social upheaval that the Court felt would have resulted in the immediate implementation of the decision. Thus the interests of southerners were favored over that of black children. This resulted in hundreds of thousands of black children, even up to the present time, being denied educational equality. Blacks still have to resort to the courts to obtain what was legally ruled to be theirs in 1954.

Many schools remain segregated. Many that were finally integrated after long, arduous struggles, began the process of resegregating. The process is particularly acute in the inner city, where black children often leave school as functional illiterates. Although progress has been made in integrating institutions of higher education, often predominantly white schools are unwilling to address themselves to the special needs of black students who have had to experience the inadequate educational systems. There will be a continued need for black institutions of higher education as long as black students are denied equal educational opportunity, and until inequities are eliminated from our society. The desegregation mandate should not be used to force black institutions to close, leaving a vacuum in place of their services.

The struggle for equality was not limited to the area of education only. After the *Brown* decision, blacks were encouraged to seek redress of their grievances in other areas. What has been described as the "Negro Revolution" began when a tired, indignant, black woman refused to give in, and did not relinquish her seat to a white man on a bus. The nation's reaction to the Civil Rights movement has been called by some, the "Second Reconstruction."

THE CIVIL RIGHTS MOVEMENT AND THE FEDERAL GOVERNMENT

The break in the separate but equal doctrine spurred black leaders to continue the assault in other areas. In December 1955, Mrs. Rosa Parks refused to go to the back of the bus in Montgomery, Alabama. She was arrested and a one-day boycott by blacks followed. The black community decided to maintain the boycott until there was complete integration of the buses. Led by the then young minister, Dr. Martin Luther King, Jr., the black community continued the boycott for over a year. They used car pools, cabs, and even walked for the right to have desegregated buses. The surge of this movement had a great impact on all the country, and it displayed the unrelenting desire of black people to end discrimination. King advocated a four-pronged attack combining direct nonviolent action, legal redress, the vote, and economic boycott. King toured the South and lectured on his philosophy of nonviolence. The movement expanded and influenced the actions of many.[34]

While the Congress of Racial Equality had used the sit-ins during the 1940s, the momentum of the 1950s gave the sit-in movement more decisive influence. In 1960, four students of North Carolina A & T State College were refused lunch counter service by a local variety store, but they continued to sit at the counter until the store closed. The sit-in movement spread throughout the South and North. The involvement of large numbers of students gave rise to the Student Nonviolent Coordinating Committee.[35] The emergence of SNCC is important in that many of the students in this organization attended black institutions of higher education and used their education in the service of the black community to break down the barriers of segregation.

The tactic of direct action in the early 1960s by the Congress of Racial Equality, the Southern Christian Leadership Conference, and the Student Nonviolent Coordinating Committee brought results and indicated the extreme hatred that some whites held toward blacks. In the name of the law, blacks were spit upon, beaten, harassed, hosed-down, shocked by cattle prods, shot, and bombed. The nation should never forget the picture of the bodies of four little girls after whites bombed their church in Birmingham, Alabama. Nor should they forget the black civil rights worker, James Chaney, and two of the many liberal white workers, Michael Schwerner and Andrew Goodman, who were killed in Mississippi, and of course, Sammy Younge, the first black student to die in the civil rights struggle.[36]

Since students were actively involved in the civil rights movement, it was inevitable that institutions of higher education would come under attack. It has already been shown how consistently racism has been reflected in discriminatory practices against blacks in higher education, and how the burden of black education fell to the private and publicly supported Negro schools. Although the Supreme Court had opened white graduate and professional schools to black students prior to the *Brown* decision, such states as Alabama and Mississippi were diehards in their opposition to their black citizens attending state universities. The lone black admitted to the University of Alabama was pelted with stones and expelled by the Board of Regents when she criticized the university for attempting to keep her from enrolling. Governor George Wallace, in 1963, physically attempted to block the entrance of three black students, in vain, by standing in the doorway of the university, and it took the presence of the National Guard to gain entrance to the University of Mississippi for James Meredith in 1962.[37]

On August 28, 1963,[38] over two hundred thousand people gathered in Washington, D.C., to protest racial inequality and to petition for a redress of grievances. The same day, Martin Luther King, Jr. announced to black and white Americans, during the "March on Washington," that he had a dream:

Now is the time to make real the promises of democracy. Now is the time to rise from the dark and desolate valley of segregation to the sunlit path of racial justice. Now is the time to lift our nation from the quicksands of racial injustice to the solid rock of brotherhood. Now is the time to make justice a reality for all God's children.

There will be neither rest nor tranquility in America until the Negro is granted his citizenship rights. The whirlwinds of revolt will continue to shake the foundations of our nation until the bright day of justice emerges.

There are those who are asking the devotees of civil rights, "When will you be satisfied?" We can never be satisfied as long as the Negro is the victim of the unspeakable horrors of police brutality. We can never be satisfied as long as our bodies, heavy with the fatigue of travel, cannot gain lodging in the motels of the highways and the hotels of the cities.

We can never be satisfied as long as our children are stripped of their selfhood and robbed of their dignity by signs saying "for whites only." We cannot be satisfied as long as the Negro in Mississippi cannot vote and the Negro in New York believes he has nothing for which to vote.

Now, I say to you today, my friends, so even though we face the difficulties of today and tomorrow, I still have a dream. It is a dream deeply rooted in the American dream. I have a dream that one day this nation will rise up and live out the true meaning of its creed: "We hold these truths to be self-evident, that all men are created equal."[39]

But before the national government could respond, the following fall in Dallas, Texas, President John F. Kennedy was assassinated.[40]

During the 1960s, Congress finally began to act and passed significant legislation to end discrimination in employment, voting, and housing. The civil rights movement as well as the riots which occurred during the sixties played an important part in convincing Congress that the continued deprivation of blacks was unhealthy for the entire nation.

Until 1964, southern legislators had been quite effective in preventing Congress from enacting any meaningful civil rights legislation. In 1957, Congress passed the first civil rights law since 1875. The Civil Rights Act of 1957 elevated the Civil Rights Section of the Department of Justice to division status. The law also created the United States Commission on Civil Rights. The commission was established as a temporary, independent, bipartisan agency directed to investigate complaints of discrimination. The commission was also charged with the responsibility to make investigations, conduct studies and submit its reports, findings, and recommendations to the President and Congress. Although the commission has produced a wide variety of excellent reports, it was not given enforcement powers to implement its recommendations. The voting provision of the act allowed the federal government to bring suits to obtain injunctive relief when a person's right to vote was denied or threatened. The Civil Rights Act of 1960 permitted the appointment of referees by federal judges to supervise elections and enroll black voters if a pattern of discriminatory treatment could be shown. Local records were subject to federal inspection on demand by federal authorities.[41]

Violence, economic reprisals, and intimidation were rampant throughout the South. Blacks were excluded from the polls through the use of poll tax, gerrymandering, and a host of other mechanisms. After Lyndon B. Johnson assumed the presidency, he urged Congress to pass the Civil Rights Bill recommended by the late President Kennedy. The Civil Rights Act of 1964 became the most comprehensive civil rights measure ever passed by Congress.[42]

Title I of the act prohibited persons from denying individuals the right to vote. This section banned the use of literacy tests unless given to everyone in writing. Title II provided injunctive relief against discrimination in places of public accommodations. Title IV provided for federal assistance in desegregating school systems. Title VI banned discrimination in federally assisted programs. Title VII provided for equal employment opportunity; discrimination based on race, color, religion, sex, or national origin was declared unlawful employment practice. This section was to be implemented over a three-year period, and it was for this purpose that the Equal Employment Opportunity Commission was created, but enforcement was to be carried out by the attorney general. Title X established the Community Relations Service as part of the Department of Commerce to assist communities in solving problems relating to discriminatory practices based on race, color, or national origin.[43]

Before the year ended, the Supreme Court, in *Heart of Atlanta Motel* v. *United States* and *Katzenbach* v. *McClung,* had declared the Civil Rights Act of 1964 constitutional. The same year, the Twenty-fourth Amendment to the Constitution was ratified, which banned the use of the poll tax in federal elections. Two years later the Supreme Court, in *Harper* v. *Virginia,* declared the poll tax in state elections unconstitutional because it violated the equal protection clause of the Fourteenth Amendment.[44]

On the heels of the 1964 Civil Rights Act, Congress passed the Voting Rights Act of 1965. The violent deaths of the Reverend James Reeb and Mrs. Viola Liuzzo during the march on Montgomery, Alabama, convinced the nation of the need for additional voting rights legislation. In states or counties where patterns of discrimination existed, the act provided for the assignment of federal examiners to register voters and observe voting procedures. The act applied to Alabama, Alaska, Georgia, Louisiana, Mississippi, South Carolina, and Virginia and twenty-six counties in North Carolina.[45]

Congress, responding to external pressure, passed additional civil rights legislation in 1968. Some southern states had proceeded to evade the Voting Rights Act of 1965 by using elections-at-large instead of district elections; consolidating predominantly black counties with predominantly white counties. as well as providing for reapportionment and redistricting. Black voters were still subject to harassment and intimidation. The Civil Rights Act of 1968 imposed criminal penalties on anyone who interfered with voters, those seeking elective office, or poll watchers. The act failed to include campaign workers or economic intimidation, which limited its effectiveness.[46]

The open-housing section of the 1968 act banned discrimination in the sale and rental of houses and apartments. The law excluded owner-sold single homes and units of four or less owner-occupied apartments. Moreover, in June, 1968 the Supreme Court in *Jones* v. *Mayer Co.,* basing its decision on the 1866 Civil Rights Act, barred all racial discrimination in the sale or rental of property.[47]

The Equal Employment Opportunity Act of 1972 filled in some of the gaps and inadequacies of previous federal legislation. For the first time, public and private educational institutions, state and local governments, and employers and unions with eight or more workers (one year after enactment) were covered by federal legislation barring discrimination and were brought under the purview of the Equal Employment Opportunity Commission (EEOC). The commission was given authority to have its decisions enforced in the courts. A serious weakness of the act was the failure of Congress to provide the commission with "cease and desist" power.[48]

The civil rights movement produced an arsenal of important legislation designed to eliminate discrimination and provide equality for blacks. Just how well did the federal government use its powers to achieve equality? In 1971, the United States Commission on Civil Rights issued *Federal Civil Rights Enforcement Effort,* a mammoth study, in which the commission concluded that the massive array of federal laws and policies achieved some success in preventing the denial of basic rights, but social and economic injustices had been allowed to grow and fester for years and the nation had just begun to deal with them. Discrimination in education, employment, and housing, the study averred, persists and "the goal of equal opportunity is far from achievement."[49]

Two years later the commission released *The Federal Civil Rights Enforcement Effort—A Reassessment* in which it concluded that the federal effort was highly inadequate. Further, the commission stated:

> In this, our most recent assessment, we have found that the inertia of agencies in the area of civil rights has persisted. In no agency did we find enforcement being accorded the priority and high-level commitment that is essential if civil rights programs are to become fully effective. Significant agency actions frequently are accompanied by extensive delays—in the issuance of regulations, and, greatest of all, in the use of sanctions when discrimination is found. Innovative steps occur here and there, but they are uncoordinated with those of other agencies.
>
> There is no Government-wide plan for civil rights enforcement. There is not even effective coordination between agencies with similar responsibilities in, for example, the employment area, where the Civil Service Commission, the Equal Employment Opportunity Commission, and the Office of Federal Contract Compliance share enforcement duties. The Equal Employment Opportunity Coordinating Council, created by Congress in March 1972 for this precise purpose, had not addressed any substantive issues in the first six months of its existence.[50]

The commission found that its latest study reinforced its earlier findings; that the efforts of the federal government in civil rights were not only inadequate but not even close to adequate. The commission found the problem to be critical because of the fundamental nature of the human rights involved—a decent job, an adequate place to live, and a suitable education. The agency further emphasized the clear moral and constitutional obligation of the federal government to end large-scale discriminatory racial practices. The commission expressed its hope for the future and then suggested that:

> The first requirement of any such effort on the part of the Chief Executive and his appointees is that of an unequivocal, forceful implementation of all the civil rights laws now on the books.
>
> In the past, the government's vast resources frequently have been effectively marshaled to cope with natural disasters, economic instability, and outbreaks of crime. Can we afford to do less when dealing with this country's greatest malignancy—racial and ethnic injustice?
>
> The answer is clearly ''no.'' But days pass into weeks, then into

months, and finally into years, and Federal civil rights enforcement proceeds at a snail's pace. It lacks creativity, resources, a sense of urgency, a firmness in dealing with violators, and most important—a sense of commitment. Time is running out on the dream of our forebears.[51]

THE ECONOMIC PLIGHT OF BLACK PEOPLE: THE CONTEMPORARY SCENE

On March 1, 1968, the "Report of the National Advisory Commission on Civil Disorders" was issued. The report concluded that "Our Nation is moving toward two societies, one black, one white—separate and un-equal."[52] Because the report accurately described the plight of black people and the causes, it was ignored by President Nixon and President Johnson before him. It is important, however, to reexamine today the causes of the urban riots of the mid-sixties because the causes still not only exist but are amplified by the present economic recession-inflationary condition.

In asking why the riots occurred, the commission found that "white racism is essentially responsible for the explosive mixture which has been accumulating in our cities since the end of World War II." Among the ingredients leading to the explosion, the commission found, were:

Pervasive discrimination and segregation in employment, education, and housing, which have resulted in the continuing exclusion of great numbers of Negroes from the benefits of economic progress.

Black in-migration and white exodus, which have produced the massive and growing concentrations of impoverished Negroes in our major cities, creating a growing crisis of deteriorating facilities and services and unmet human needs.

The black ghettos, where segregation and poverty converge on the young to destroy opportunity and enforce failure. Crime, drug addiction, dependency on welfare, and bitterness and resentment against society in general and white society in particular are the result.

At the same time, most whites and some Negroes outside the ghetto have prospered to a degree unparalled in the history of civilization. Through television and other media, this influence has been flaunted before the eyes of the Negro poor and the jobless ghetto youth.[53]

The report found that these factors did not by themselves cause the riots. Blacks were frustrated by the initial progress of the civil rights movement and the unfulfilled dreams sparked by favorable Supreme Court decisions and legislative victories. White terrorism directed against nonviolent protestors had created a climate which encouraged violence as a form of protest. This process was abetted by the open defiance of federal law and authority by state and local officials as they resisted efforts to desegregate. Young blacks, who exhibited increased racial consciousness and pride, were no longer willing to accept the status quo. They often resented the police who in this instance served as the "spark factor" in causing the riot and who symbolized white power. "The atmosphere of hostility and cynicism is reinforced by a widespread belief among Negroes in the existence of police brutality and in a 'double standard' of justice and protection—one for Negroes and one for whites."[54]

The commission found that life in the ghetto for blacks was strikingly different from life experienced by white residents of middle-class suburbs. Between 2 million and 2.5 million blacks live in "squalor and deprivation" in ghetto neighborhoods. Even as the economy grew and general unemployment declined, the unemployment rate for blacks remained twice the rate for whites in 1967, and as long as this situation continued, blacks were unable to break out of the circle of poverty. Those who managed to maintain a stable level of employment were often forced to accept the most undesirable jobs—low-paying, unskilled or service jobs. The conclusion reached was that the continued relegation of the worst jobs to black males was the single most important reason for poverty among black people. Their unemployment and underemployment reached as high as 33 percent in low income neighborhoods, or 8.8 times greater than the overall unemployment rate for all United States workers. While 11.9 percent of whites were declared below the poverty line (in 1966, $3,335 per year for an urban family of four), 40.6 percent of all nonwhite families were in poverty.[55]

This problem of poverty and unemployment had and still has a direct impact on the quality of life in the ghetto. Today the crime rate is consistently higher; thirty-five times as many serious crimes are committed against blacks in ghettos than against persons in white districts. Poor health and lack of proper nutrition cause higher mortality rates and higher incidence of major disease with fewer medical services. It was estimated that of the fourteen thousand rat bites in the United States in 1965, most occurred in the ghetto. Ghetto residents paid higher prices for goods sold in neighborhood stores, compounding the economic plight of black urban residents.[56] As part of the effort to solve the problem, the commission felt that elimination of discrimination and increased educational service played a key role. The commission suggested the following:

> Education in a democratic society must equip children to develop their potential and to participate fully in American life. For the community at large, the schools have discharged this responsibility well. But for the minorities, and particularly for the children of the ghetto, the schools have failed to provide the educational experience which could overcome the effects of discrimination and deprivation.
>
> This failure is one of the persistent sources of grievance and resentment within the Negro community. The hostility of Negro parents and students toward the school system is generating increasing conflict and causing disruption within many city school districts. But the most dramatic evidence of the relationship between educational practices and civil disorders lies in the high incidence of riot participation by ghetto youth who have not completed high school.
>
> The bleak record of public education for ghetto children is growing worse. In the critical skills—verbal and reading ability—Negro students are falling further behind whites with each year of school completed. The high unemployment rate for Negro youth is evidence, in part, of the growing educational crisis.
>
> We support integration as the priority education strategy; it is essential to the future of American society. In this last summer's disorders we have seen the consequences of racial isolation at all levels, and of attitudes toward race, on both sides, produced by three centuries of myth, ignorance, and bias. It is indispensable that opportunities for interaction between the races be expanded.
>
> We recognize that the growing dominance of pupils from disadvantaged minorities in city school populations will not soon be reversed. No matter how great the effort toward desegregation, many children of the ghettos will not, within their school careers, attend integrated schools.
>
> If existing disadvantages are not to be perpetuated, we must drastically improve the quality of ghetto education. Equality of results with all-white schools must be the goal.

The commission recommended the following to implement these strategies:

> Sharply increase efforts to eliminate de facto segregation in our schools through substantial federal aid to school systems seeking to

desegregate either within the system or in cooperation with neighboring school systems.

Elimination of racial discrimination in northern as well as southern schools by vigorous application of Title VI of the Civil Rights Act of 1964.

Extension of quality early childhood education to every disadvantaged child in the country.

Efforts to improve dramatically schools serving disadvantaged children through substantial federal funding of year-round quality compensatory education programs, improved teaching, and expanded experimentation and research.

Elimination of illiteracy through greater Federal support for adult basic education.

Enlarged opportunities for parent and community participation in the public schools.

Reoriented vocational education emphasizing work experience training and the involvement of business and industry.

Expanded opportunities for higher education through increased federal assistance to disadvantaged students.

Revision of state aid formulas to assure more per student aid to districts having a high proportion of disadvantaged school age children.[57]

Yet, by the mid-seventies, very little had been done to implement the commission's recommendations. In fact, the current recession has exacerbated the plight of black people. The most recent data on the general black population of the United States was issued in August 1975 by the Census Bureau. At best, the study indicated that the present social and economic situation for blacks is a varied picture. While limited progress was made in such fields as education, health, and election of blacks to public office in the 1970s, blacks made less economic progress, and in fact, in some areas they regressed. Black family income fell increasingly behind that of white families in this decade. In 1969, black family median income was 61 percent of white family median income, but by 1973, it had fallen to 58 percent, where it remained through 1974. When the percentages are translated into dollars, blacks received $7,808 per year as compared to $13,356 for whites. This apparent economic progress is further complicated by the fact that incomes of blacks are accrued through the combined efforts of both the husband and wife, whereas in a number of instances white family incomes reflect the earnings of the husband only, although this is changing as more white females seek jobs.[58]

The outlook for immediate black economic progress is not good. The Gross National Product has continued to decline into 1975. While the purchasing power of American workers steadily declined, the number of unemployed increased by 48 percent from 5.6 million to 8.3 million from the fourth quarter in 1974 to the first quarter in 1975. As of March 1975, 105 of 150 major metropolitan labor areas had 6 percent or more unemployment.[59]

While the general economic condition of the nation was poor, the plight of blacks reached crisis proportions. Black workers without jobs reached an all-time high of 1.45 million during the first quarter of 1975. The rate of black unemployment increased from 10.9 percent to 14.2 percent. Black workers were so discouraged by the present economic situation that during the first quarter of 1975, 107,000 of them gave up looking for work. The fact that so many blacks so completely drop out of the labor market led to a report on the hidden unemployed by the National Urban League. The league discovered 2.93 million black unemployed workers, more than double the official rate. Thus the unofficial unemployment rate for blacks during the first quarter of 1975 was 25.8 percent, up from 21.1 percent during the fourth quarter of 1974. In other words, the black unemployment rate increased from 1 out of every 5 to 1 of every 4 workers. The league calculated that white unemployment actually rose from 10.8 percent to 14.6 percent.[60]

While the National Urban League concluded that the plight of the nation was much more than the official reports revealed, the plight of black people was substantially worse. For example, the official unemployment rate for residents of poverty areas was 16.4 percent; the league's unofficial estimate places the rate at three times the official estimate and in some areas over 50 percent. To further compound the problem, black men were hardest hit during the first quarter of 1975, accounting for three-fifths of the decline in unemployed blacks. Black married men experienced an unemployment increase of double what it had been in the fourth quarter of 1974, rising from 5 percent to 9.8 percent by the first quarter of 1975. The official rate for black teenage males jumped to 38.1 percent during the first quarter of 1975, while the rate for black teenage females soared to 14.3 percent.[61]

Blacks were more likely to remain unemployed over longer periods of time than were whites. Blacks were also more likely than were whites to remain permanently outside the labor market because of their inability to obtain employment. To further complicate the black economic situation, six hundred two thousand black workers were ineligible for unemployment compensation.[62]

The Urban League came to the following conclusion:

The unemployment situation for all Americans workers but especially for blacks, was devastating during the first three months of 1975. Even the official unemployment figures are at their highest levels since the Great Depression of the 1930s. The rate of inflation has "normalized" at such a high level that the Bureau of Labor Statistics now estimates that a family of four needed $9,200 in the autumn of 1974 to maintain its *lower* standard of living! And prices have steadily risen since then.

Adult male breadwinners are being laid off their jobs in virtually all sectors of the economy at a record-setting pace and are remaining out of work for longer and longer periods of time. Women heads of households and working wives are being forced to drop out or stay out of the labor force, at a time when their contribution to the economic status of the family is most needed. And teenagers, especially blacks, are becoming so discouraged that thousands of them have given up actively seeking work—just when their supplemental economic support is vital to many low income families.

Yet, many public officials and economists are declaring that the "worst is over," that we are "bottoming out" and "on the road to recovery."

If the nation is on the road to recovery, then past experience clearly indicates that the black community will remain in recession long after the rest of the country has been restored to prosperity—unless a genuine national commitment is made to improve the economic situation of *all* Americans.

But, instead, many analysts are already asserting that the economy may have to stabilize at a six percent level of unemployment in order to avert a resurgence of inflation. They have yet to indicate what the "tolerable" official level of unemployment for blacks would be at this new level of "full" employment—11 or 12 percent?

It is imperative that the principles set forth at the Black Economic Summit meeting in the fall of 1974 be heeded by all:
"There is no tolerable level of unemployment. One of the success measures of any economy or system of government is its ability to provide meaningful jobs in the public and private sector at an equitable and adequate wage for all citizens who are willing and able to work. Full employment is our goal."[63]

The future of black Americans will be bleak unless positive action is initiated now to correct the present inequity. The historical analysis of the plight of black people in this country illustrates that their plight is not merely a result of the current recession. It is the result of deliberate, conscious decisions on the part of power-holders to keep blacks at the bottom levels of American society. The recession is exacerbating an already intolerable situation, doubling and tripling the rate of unemployment for black subgroups. What must be clearly perceived and understood is that without special efforts to aid the black masses, a general recovery in the economy will not, by the very nature of the system, result in a corresponding general recovery of the black economic situation. A recovery without special assistance will result in the traditional black double unemployment rate over whites which some policymakers have, from all indications, determined is acceptable. Thus if the black economic situation is to improve in any permanent way, the nation must commit itself to an increased emphasis on affirmative action for blacks—even at a time of national recession. Only through this commitment will blacks recover to the extent that the nation recovers. Only through such an affirmative approach will black unemployment rates stabilize at the same rate for the whole country instead of a possible 11 or even 12 percent.

THE LEGAL BASIS FOR AFFIRMATIVE ACTION

Affirmative action is well-grounded in American modern history and has a sound basis in law, in spite of the inadequate nature of efforts to eliminate discriminatory practices. The basis for the prohibition of discrimination in federally financed or assisted programs began under President Franklin D. Roosevelt and his New Deal. After a threat by A. Philip Randolph to march on Washington, Roosevelt issued Executive Order 8802 in June 1941, which established the Committee on Fair Employment Practices. The committee investigated complaints of discrimination it received against companies with government defense contracts. Executive Order 9346 (May 1943) expanded the program to include more industries and extended the coverage to require that employers and labor unions not discriminate in hiring, in providing tenure and terms and conditions of employment. The program was effectively terminated when Congress failed to continue the committee's funds.[64]

Throughout the 1950s and middle 1960s, presidents issued numerous executive orders, but all generally lacked effective mechanisms for enforcement. President Harry S. Truman issued Executive Order 10308 (December

1951) which set up a Committee on Government Contract Compliance (CGCC). All government contractors signed nondiscrimination clauses which were enforced by the funding agencies, but administration was left to CGCC. Although President Dwight D. Eisenhower's Executive Order 10479 (August 1953) and 10557 (September 1954) extended the coverage, the committee's lack of enforcement powers left it basically as an advisory-supervisory body chaired by Vice-President Richard M. Nixon.[65]

When President John F. Kennedy took office, he issued on March 6, 1961, Executive Order 10925 and later Executive Order 11114, which established the President's Committee on Equal Employment Opportunity (CEEO) with responsibility for ending discrimination by government contractors as well as all agencies within the federal government itself. The CEEO was also given authority over federally assisted construction projects with power to debar any contractor out of compliance. For the first time, a committee with a sufficient budget to make an impact was given the responsibility to attack systemic discrimination through affirmative action. Yet significant changes were never brought about because the penalty provisions were never employed.[66]

The heart of the government nondiscrimination compliance program was firmly established by Executive Order 11246 issued by President Lyndon B. Johnson, September 1965, as amended by Executive Order 11375 (October 1967) and 11478 (August 1969). Overall responsibility for the implementation of Executive Order 11246 is lodged with the Secretary of Labor who, in January 1966, established the Office of Federal Contract Compliance (OFCC). Executive Order 11246 is implemented by OFCC regulations which are in two parts: (1) obligations of contractors and subcontractors not to discriminate and (2) contractors' obligation to develop an affirmative action program. The nondiscrimination concept in 11246 requires that any and all discriminatory conditions relating to employment be eliminated. The affirmative action requirement means that employers will do more than remain neutral, but will undertake a special effort to recruit, employ and promote qualified members of groups that had heretofore been excluded, even if excluded inadvertently.[67] Since neutrality in hiring would only perpetuate the status quo indefinitely, affirmative action is designed to overcome the effects of systemic institutionalization of discrimination and exclusion.

Affirmative action, as listed in Revised Order No. 4, requires a contractor to determine whether or not he has employed a representative number of minorities and women and to establish goals and timetables to overcome any deficiency of minority representation. Thus a part of the affirmative action program must consist of establishing the number of available minorities and women in a given job category; after an estimable number of qualified minorities and job openings within the company has been determined, the contractor must project how many qualified minorities and women may be hired. The employer must adopt genuine and effective techniques and procedures for locating minorities and women and eliminate racial discrimination within the structure and operation of the institution.[68]

The OFCC has overall responsibility for the government's contract compliance program, but has delegated primary responsibility to various federal agencies. The Department of Health, Education, and Welfare Office for Civil Rights (OCR) has been delegated compliance authority by OFCC to enforce the provisions of the Executive Order in institutions of higher education. In fiscal year 1971, 2,368 institutions of higher education received $3.48 billion from 14 federal agencies (HEW contributed 65 percent of this amount). In 1972, HEW awarded over $2.84 billion in grants and contracts to colleges and universities. These institutions are thus required to comply with federal civil rights requirements.[69]

AFFIRMATIVE ACTION AND HIGHER EDUCATION

Affirmative action should be utilized in all aspects of American employment, but especially in the area of education. Education has traditionally been used as a mechanism for upward mobility. Until recently, educational institutions have been among the last bastions of segregation and employment discrimination. Of all blacks between the ages of eighteen and twenty-four, 15% were enrolled in college in 1970 while 18% were enrolled in 1974. For whites in this age range college enrollment went down from 27% in 1970 to 25% in 1974. For whites, all of the decline in proportional enrollment was experienced by males, while for blacks, the greater increase in proportional college enrollment was experienced by males. Although the enrollment of blacks in higher education has improved, the barriers to access, distribution, and enrollment, as evidenced by the low proportional enrollment must be removed.[70]

One could easily assume that enlightened university communities would have implemented basic federal affirmative action requirements and even surpassed them without any difficulty. But instead, institutions of higher education have been the most vocal of all groups that have renounced the federal affirmative action program. As of April 1975, HEW had approved only thirty-two affirmative action plans, one of which was the University of California at Berkeley plan, the only one to date given final approval by the Department of Labor.[71]

The Berkeley affirmative action plan is an example of how complicated federal procedures can be used to obscure the real goal of removing the effects of past discrimination. Under pressure from HEW, Berkeley followed the detailed requirements of the executive order regulations. After spending $300,000 and using complicated statistical analyses, the university concluded, with the approval of the federal bureaucracy, that over a thirty-year period only one black and three Asian Americans would have to be added to the faculty to achieve the university's affirmative action goal. It is obvious from an analysis of this and other affirmative action plans that results do not necessarily occur from strict adherence to the letter of the law, but rather from a commitment to the spirit of the law.[72]

In addition to the problems inherent in the administration of affirmative action programs and the attacks on these programs by institutions of higher education, there are the recent attacks by scholars on the inability of blacks to take advantage of opportunities in higher education. Historically, these attacks on black intelligence, which began as early as colonial times, were used to justify slavery and black economic exploitation. They are once again being resurrected as blacks begin to seek a more equitable representation at all levels of higher education.

It is evident that since 1954, some progress has been made, but not close to the progress that should have been made to eliminate systemic discrimination. For decades, blacks used the judiciary in their efforts to seek redress. The Supreme Court made significant advances toward the goal of social justice, and these advances were followed by the more hesitant and often reluctant efforts of the executive and legislative branches of government. But the attack on the institutionalization of racism has yet to be made. An aggressive commitment to affirmative action is one way to achieve true equality of opportunity and to reverse nearly four hundred years of racism.

CONCLUSION

This brief narrative has succinctly documented how white Americans have consistently and systematically denied black Americans their basic human rights. The process began with the colonization of the New World when colonists from western Europe discovered that they needed cheap labor to exploit the vast resources of the Americas. Labor shortages led first to the exploitation of poor whites and Indians, until the introduction of black Africans provided an alternative. The physical differences between blacks and whites, coupled with the ethnocentrism of Europeans, led to the enslavement of Africans. Europeans quickly inferred that the differences between them and Africans were due to blacks' racial and cultural inferiority. This alleged inferiority allowed for the development of an elaborate system of race prejudice and discrimination which perpetuated race distinctions.

Racial and ethnic discrimination in America have not only affected blacks, but many groups, especially immigrants, have faced discrimination in one form or another. This leads some to argue, then why provide special compensation for black people? The answer is firmly rooted in American history.

Black Americans suffered and continued to suffer the social degradation no other group in America experienced. They were the only Americans who were enslaved and on whose labor a civilization developed. The institution of slavery was sanctioned and protected by the United States Constitution. The legal protection for slavery offered by the Constitution was so powerful that even Abraham Lincoln, the Great Emancipator, preferred to provide economic compensation to slaveholders rather than free the slaves outright and thus violate the right of property slaveholders held to enslave blacks. In addition to the disabling features of slavery, the vast majority of states denied free blacks the right of citizenship and even developed an elaborate system of discriminatory laws to assure that blacks remain at the bottom of society. Finally, the most serious detriment occurred in 1857 when the Supreme Court ruled that blacks were not and could never be citizens of the United States under the Constitution. With the exception of American Indians, no other group has ever been so excluded.

Although slavery had divided the nation, eventually leading to a civil war, there was not unanimity over the extension of citizenship to the freedmen after the war. For a brief period, constitutional amendments were adopted and legislation was passed favorable to the ex-slaves. The slaves were freed, made American citizens and guaranteed all the privileges and immunities enjoyed by white Americans. A few statesmen realized that after generations of deprivation, special compensatory programs were necessary if blacks were to adequately compete with the more privileged majority. The most promising act passed established the Bureau of Refugees, Freedmen and Abandoned Lands.

After performing a remarkable job with limited resources, the bureau was disbanded. Within less than a decade, the nation quickly tired of "waving the bloody shirt." Conservative whites, who had fought against the United States, gained control over their states and local governments through violence and intimidation, when other means failed. The Supreme Court, reflecting the mood of the nation, began, through a series of historic decisions, to negate the few measures passed by Congress to protect the freedmen. Their decisions culminated in the infamous *Plessy* v. *Ferguson* decision of 1896 which gave official sanction to segregation and second-class citizenship for blacks. Black people were once again deprived of their rights. They were the only group that was systematically denied its rights through violence and the sanction of law.

The abiding faith black people have had in education, and their dedication to the principles of democracy and justice, did little to alter racial hostility. The freedmen and their white allies established the foundation for free, publicly supported education in the South, only to be denied an equal opportunity to share in that system. In most other instances, blacks were denied education.

Blacks have never given up hope that one day equality would be extended to them. They were heartened by the 1954 Supreme Court *Brown* decision which ushered in the civil rights revolution. The Court's decision barring segregation in public schools brought encouragement to blacks and made them feel that they, too, would be included in the American Dream. During the 1960s and 1970s blacks made a number of gains, but soon realized that what the nation finally conceded as rightfully theirs had been promised to them over one hundred years ago with the adoption of the Thirteenth, Fourteenth, and Fifteenth Amendments and various civil rights acts. Furthermore, the early 1970s witnessed a recession-depression that caused blacks to lose much of what they had the gained during the previous decade.

This narrative has illustrated that for over three and one-half centuries, white Americans have consistently discriminated against black Americans. The nation has run the gamut from the blatant cruelty of slavery to the more subtle forms of discrimination practiced today. It is evident that sustained support for aggressive affirmative action enforcement is necessary if the cyclical-effect of race discrimination is to be eliminated. Just as slavery had become institutionalized, so has race prejudice become systemic. Affirmative action will not alleviate all of the problems, but strong implementation of affirmative action, especially in higher education, can do much to assure a more equitable distribution of opportunity. If this country, as it celebrates two hundred years of freedom for some of its citizens, is to eradicate racism, it has to be prepared to institute genuine integration of the races.

Affirmative efforts to bring black people into the mainstream of American life will have a direct influence on the quality of life for all Americans over the next two hundred years. The true goal of affirmative action is not to deny opportunities to those who presently are dominant, but to see that each person has the opportunity to achieve his or her full potential and to bring to the whole society the wealth found in cultural diversity. Colleges and universities are institutions designed to educate America's youth, but just as tomorrow's youth will have to live in a world made up of different races and sexes, so must the nature of students' education reflect the composition of the country if they are going to adequately solve the problems of tomorrow. Affirmative action thus provides the under-represented an opportunity to achieve their full potential while giving the larger society the variety found in different, but rich, cultural experiences.

NOTES

CHAPTER I

1.   Edgar J. McManus, *A History of Negro Slavery in New York* (Syracuse: Syracuse University Press, 1966), p. 3; Gilbert C. Fite and Jim C. Reese, *An Economic History of the United States* (Boston: Houghton Mifflin, 1965), p. 35.

2.   August Meier and Elliot Rudwick, *From Plantation to Ghetto, An Interpretive History of American Negroes* (New York: Hill and Wang, Inc., 1966), p. 36; Louis M. Hacker, *The Triumph of American Capitalism* (New York: Simon and Schuster, 1940), pp. 97-103; Lorenzo T. Greene, *The Negro in Colonial New England, 1620-1776* (New York: Columbia University Press, 1942), pp. 18-19; Benjamin Brawley, *A Social History of the American Negro* (New York: Collier Books, 1970), pp. 91-95.

3.   Joel A. Rogers, *Africa's Gift to America* (New York: Helga M. Rogers, 1961), p. 37; Brawley, *A Social History*, p. 93.

4.   Greene, *The Negro*, p. 19; Winthrop Jordan, *White Over Black: American Attitudes Toward The Negro, 1550-1812* (Baltimore: Penguin Books, Inc., 1969), pp. 86-89.

5.   McManus, *Negro Slavery*, pp. 1, 4; Greene, *The Negro*, p. 21.

6. Harold D. Woodman, ed., *Slavery and the Southern Economy* (New York: Harcourt, Brace and World, 1966), p. 2.

7. Eric Williams, *Capitalism and Slavery* (Chapel Hill: University of North Carolina Press, 1944), p. 78.

8. W. E. B. DuBois, *The Suppression of the African Slave Trade to the United States of America, 1638-1870* (New York: Dover Publications, Inc., 1970), pp. 27-29.

9. Kenneth M. Stampp, *The Peculiar Institution: Slavery in the Ante-Bellum South* (New York: Vintage Books, 1956), pp. 3, 5.

10. *Ibid*, p. 24.

11. William Sumner Jenkins, *Pro-Slavery Thought in the Old South* (Gloucester, Massachusetts: Peter Smith, 1960), pp. 1-2.

12. *Ibid.*, p. 13.

13. *Ibid.*, pp. 15, 17.

14. *Ibid.*, pp. 23, 31-32; Benjamin Quarles, *The Negro in the American Revolution* (Chapel Hill: The University of North Carolina Press, 1961), p. vii.

15. Herbert Aptheker, *American Negro Slave Revolts* (New York: International Publishers, 1969), pp. 106, 269-76, 293-324; Benjamin Quarles, *Black Abolitionists* (New York: Oxford University Press, 1969), p. 17; See also Charles M. Wiltse, ed., *David Walker's Appeal to Colored Citizens of the World* (New York: Hill and Wang, Inc., 1965).

16. Jenkins, *Pro-Slavery*, pp. 65-66, 78, 89-90; Eric L. McKitrick, ed., *Slavery Defended: The Views of the Old South* (Englewood Cliffs, New Jersey: Prentice Hall, 1963), pp. 2, 6, 20, 34, 86, 139.

17. Jenkins, *Pro-Slavery*, pp. 200-203, 208-9, 216, 243-44, 250-51.

18. Stampp, *The Peculiar Institution*, pp. 156-62.

19. *Ibid.*, pp. 208, 313-24.

20. *Ibid.*, pp. 144-48; Carter G. Woodson, *The Education of the Negro Prior to 1861* (New York: Arno Press and *The New York Times*, 1968), pp. 1-2.

21. Jordan, *White Over Black*, pp. 43-44, 71-72, 75, 79.

22. *Ibid.*, pp. 104-106.

23. Brawley, *Social History*, pp. 14-42; Aptheker, *Slave Revolts*, pp. 187-89.

24. John F. Grimke, compiler, *The Public Laws of the State of*

South Carolina From Its First Establishment as a British Province Down to the Year 1790 (Philadelphia: R. Aitken and Sons, 1790), pp. 163-74.

25.   John C. Hurd, *The Law of Freedom and Bondage in the United States,* Vol. I (New York: Negro Universities Press, 1968), pp. 232, 268.

26.   Jordan, *White over Black,* pp. 270-271.

27.   Quarles, *The Negro,* p. vii.

28.   *Ibid.,* pp. 199-200.

29.   U. S., *Constitution,* Art. I. Sec. 2, 9; Art. IV, Sec 2.

30.   Loren Miller, *The Petitioners: The Story of the Supreme Court of The United States and the Negro* (Cleveland: World Publishing Company, 1966), p. 21.

31.   Hacker, *American Capitalism,* p. 166; Fite, *An Economic History,* p. 117.

32.   Hacker, *American Capitalism,* p. 287; Woodman, *Slavery,* pp. 2-4.

33.   Woodman, *Slavery,* pp. 2-4; Albert N. O. Brooks, "Education of the Negro in Virginia Prior to 1861" (Master of Arts thesis, Howard University, Washington, D.C., 1938), pp. 31-32.

34.   Brooks, "Education," p. 32; Woodson, *The Education,* pp. 152-53.

35.   Woodman, *Slavery,* pp. 4-5; Douglas North, *The Economic Growth of the United States, 1790-1860,* (Englewood Cliffs, New Jersey: Prentice-Hall, 1961), p. 52.

36.   Woodman, *Slavery,* p. 5.

37.   Charles S. Sydnor, *Slavery in Mississippi* (Baton Rouge: Louisiana State University Press, 1966), pp. 181-82.

38.   Henry W. Farnam, *Chapters in the History of Social Legislation in the United States to 1860* (Washington, D.C.: Carnegie Institution of Washington, 1938), pp. 182-84.

39.   *Ibid.,* pp. 187-98.

40.   *Ibid.,* p. 193.

41.   William Goodell, *The American Slave Code in Theory and in Practice* (London: Clarke, Beeton and Co., 1853), pp. 319-22.

42.   Wiltse, *David Walker's Appeal,* pp. vii-x.

43.   Aptheker, *Slave Revolts,* pp. 293-302.

44.   Hurd, *The Law,* II, p. 9.

45.   Goodell, *Slave Code,* p. 323.

46.   *Ibid.,* p. 324.

47. Miller, *The Petitioners*, pp. 9-11.

48. Leon F. Litwack, *North of Slavery: The Negro in the Free States*, 1790-1860 (Chicago: The University of Chicago Press, 1961), pp. 30-31.

49. *Ibid.*, pp. 31-32.

50. Jordan, *White Over Black*, pp. 328-30.

51. Alfred H. Kelly and Winfred A. Harbison, *The American Constitution: Its Origins and Development* (New York: W.W. Norton and Co., 1963), pp. 268-70.

52. Litwack, *North of Slavery*, pp. 74-78.

53. Vincent C. Hopkins, *Dred Scott's Case* (New York: Fordham University Press, 1951), pp. 61-76.

54. Litwack, *North of Slavery*, pp. 93-94, 97, 100-101.

55. "Eighteenth Century Petition of South Carolina Negroes," *Journal of Negro History* XXXI (1946), 98-99; Guion G. Johnson, *Ante-Bellum North Carolina, A Social History* (Chapel Hill: University of North Carolina Press, 1937), pp. 585, 598; John Lofton, *Insurrection in South Carolina* (Yellow Springs, Ohio: Antioch Press, 1964), pp. 155-83.

56. Stanley Feldstein, *Once a Slave: The Slave's View of Slavery* (New York: William Morrow and Company, Inc., 1971), p. 61.

57. Stampp, *The Peculiar Institution*, pp. 31-32.

58. *Ibid.*, pp. 34-41.

59. *Ibid.*, pp. 44-45, 57-58.

60. Feldstein, *Once a Slave*, pp. 184-87.

61. *Ibid.*

62. *Ibid.*, pp. 62-63; John W. Blassingame, *The Slave Community: Plantation Life in the Ante-Bellum South* (New York: Oxford University Press, 1972), p. 207.

63. Stampp, *The Peculiar Institution*, pp. 58-59; Feldstein, *Once a Slave*, p. 62.

64. Stampp, *The Peculiar Institution*, p. 59.

65. Sterling D. Spero and Abram L. Harris, *The Black Worker* (New York: Atheneum, 1972), p. 5.

66. *Ibid.*, pp. 5-6; W. E. B. DuBois, ed., *Negro Artisan* (New York: Arno Press and *The New York Times*, 1969), p. 4.

67. Spero and Harris, *The Black Worker*, pp. 5-6; DuBois, *Negro Artisan*, p. 14.

68. DuBois, *Negro Artisan*, pp. 15-16; Spero and Harris, *The*

Black Worker, pp. 7-14.

69. Spero and Harris, *The Black Worker,* p.7.

70. *Ibid.,* p. 8; DuBois, *Negro Artisan,* p. 15.

71. Raymond S. Franklin and Solomon Resnik, *The Political Economy of Racism* (New York: Holt, Rinehart and Winston, 1973), 1973), p. 12.

72. Charles H. Wesley, *Negro Labor in the United States* (New York: Russell and Russell, 1967), p. 142; Sydnor, *Slavery in Mississippi,* pp. 54-55.

73. Eugene Genovese, ed., *The Slave Economics,* Vol. II (New York: John Wiley and Sons, Inc., 1973), pp. 155-56.

74. *Ibid.,* p. 156.

75. Woodson, *The Education,* p. 129.

76. Goodell, *American Slave Code,* pp. 319-325; Wiltse, *David Walker's Appeal,* pp. ix-xii.

77. Litwack, *North of Slavery,* pp. 113-14.

78. Quarles, *Black Abolitionists,* p. 110.

79. *Ibid.,* pp. 110-11.

80. *Ibid.,* pp. 114; Woodson, *The Education,* pp. 270-72.

81. Quarles, *Black Abolitionists,* p. 114.

82. Rayford W. Logan, *The Negro in the United States, Volume I: A History to 1945—From Slavery to Second-Class Citizenship* (New York: Van Nostrand, Reinhold Company, 1970), p. 9; Theodore Draper, *The Rediscovery of Black Nationalism* (New York: The Viking Press, 1969), pp. 4-5.

83. Logan, *The Negro,* I, p. 9; Draper, *Black Nationalism,* pp. 16-17.

84. Draper, *Black Nationalism,* pp. 7-8, 11.

85. *Ibid.,* pp. 7-10.

86. *Ibid.,* p. 8; Logan, *The Negro,* I,pp. 9, 10.

87. Carter G. Woodson, *Negro Orators and Their Orations* (Washington, D.C.: Associated Publishers, 1925), pp. 80-81.

88. Woodson, *The Education,* p. 257.

89. *Ibid.,* pp. 257-58.

90. *Ibid.,* p. 259.

91. Leslie H. Fishel Jr. and Benjamin Quarles, *The Black American: A Documentary History* (Glenview, Illinois: Scott, Foresman and Company, 1970), p. 168.

92. *Ibid.,* pp. 168-69; Litwack, *North of Slavery,* pp. 214-15;

Woodson, *The Education,* pp. 260-62.

93.   Litwack,*North of Slavery,* pp. 216, 221; Fishel and Quarles, *The Black American,* p. 139.

94.   Litwack, *North of Slavery,* pp. 215-16; 223-24, 226.

95.   *Ibid.,* pp. 113-14.

96.   *Ibid.,* pp. 117-19; Quarles, *Black Abolitionists,* pp. 12-13.

97.   "The Iron-Willed Black Schoolmaster and his Granite Academy," *Middlebury College News Letter* (Spring, 1974), p. 6; *Amherst Alumni News,* (Winter, 1962), p. 20; Woodson, *The Education,* p. 265.

98.   Woodson, *The Education,* pp. 266-67.

99.   *Ibid.,* pp. 271-73.

100.   Fishel and Quarles, *The Black American,* p. 172.

CHAPTER II

1.   Rayford W. Logan, *The Negro in the United States,* Vol. I (New York: Van Nostrand, Reinhold Company, 1970), pp. 17-18; Edwin C. Rozwenc, ed., *The Causes of The American Civil War* (Lexington, Massachusetts: D. C. Heath and Company, 1972), pp. 147-164, 242-266.

2.   Henry W. Wilbur, *President Lincoln's Attitude Toward Slavery and Emancipation* (New York: Bible and Tanner, 1970), pp. 42, 49, 130.

3.   *Ibid.,* pp. 27-34, 56; John Hope Franklin, *The Emancipation Proclamation* (Garden City, New York: Anchor Books, 1965), pp. 91-93, 123.

4.   Carl Schurz, *The Reminiscences of Carl Schurz,* Vol. III (New York: McClure Company, 1908), pp. 166-67, 181; John T. Trowbridge, *The Desolate South, 1865-1866,* ed. by Gordon Carroll, (New York: Duell, Sloan and Pearce, 1956), pp. 274-75; John T. Trowbridge, *The South: A Journey Through the Desolated States and Talks With the People* (Hartford, Connecticut: L. Stebbins, 1866), pp. 566-67.

5.   Trowbridge, *The South,* p. 532; Walter L. Fleming, *Documentary History of Reconstruction,* Vol. I (Cleveland: The Arthur H. Clark Co., 1906), pp. 77-78; Joel Williamson, *After Slavery: The Negro in South Carolina During Reconstruction, 1861-1877* (Chapel Hill: The University of North Carolina Press, 1965), pp. 32-33, 40.

6.   Logan, *The Negro,* I, p. 22; Theodore B. Wilson, *The Black*

Codes of The South (University, Alabama: University of Alabama Press, 1965), pp. 66-75.

7. Francis B. Simkins and Robert H. Woody, *South Carolina During Reconstruction* (Chapel Hill: The University of North Carolina Press, 1932), p. 37; *Reports and Resolutions of The South Carolina General Assembly, 1865-1866* (Columbia, S.C.: State Printing Office, n.d.), pp. 7, 13; *The Charleston Daily Courier*, September 20, 23, 25-26, 1865; Sidney Andrews, *The South Since the War* (Boston: Tickner and Fields, 1866), pp. 86-89.

8. See *Courier*, November 10, 1865; *Reports and Resolutions*, pp. 285-332; John S. Reynolds, *Reconstruction in South Carolina* (Columbia, S. C.: The State Company, 1905), pp. 167-71, 175 for a detailed discussion of the code.

9. William Goodell, *The American Slave Code in Theory and Practice* (London: Clarke, Beeton, and Co., 1854), pp. 167-80.

10. W. E. B. DuBois, *Black Reconstruction in America, 1860-1880* (Cleveland: Meridian Books, 1965), p. 641.

11. *Ibid.*, p. 646.

12. Allen W. Trelease, *White Terror: The Ku Klux Klan Conspiracy and Southern Reconstruction* (New York: Harper and Row, 1971), pp. 3, 68.

13. *Ibid.*, pp. 36, 131.

14. *Ibid.*, p. 316; Elisabeth S. Peck, *Berea's First Century, 1855-1955* (Lexington: University of Kentucky Press, 1955), pp. 2, 8, 37, 49-53.

15. Henry Wilson, *The Rise and Fall of the Slave Power in America*, Vol. III (Boston: James R. Osgood and Company, 1877), pp. 517-18.

16. Wilson, *Slave Power*, III, pp. 517-18; Reynolds, *Reconstruction*, pp. 7-8; Reynold's five theories of Reconstruction have been reduced to two here; John W. Burgess, *Reconstruction and the Constitution, 1866-1876* (New York: Charles Scribner's Sons, 1907), pp. 9-10.

17. James D. Richardson, ed., *A Compilation of The Messages and Papers of the Presidents*, Vol. VI (Washington, D.C.: Government Printing Office, 1897), pp. 276-77.

18. Wilson, *Slave Power*, p. 529.

19. Richardson, *Messages and Papers*, VI, pp. 284-85, 310-12; Alfred H. Kelly and Winfred H. Harbison, *The American Constitution*

(New York: W. W. Norton and Company, Inc., 1963), pp. 452-53; Ina Van Noppen, *The South: A Documentary History* (Princeton, N. J.: D. Van Nostrand Co., Inc., 1958), pp. 333-34.

20.   LaWanda Cox and John H. Cox, *Politics, Principles and Prejudice, 1865-1866: Dilemma of Reconstruction America* (New York: Atheneum Press, 1969), pp. 1-5.

21.   *Ibid.,* pp. 6, 22, 24-25.

22.   *Ibid.,* pp. 152-159.

23.   *Ibid.,* pp. 163-210.

24.   Loren Miller, *The Petitioners: The Story of The Supreme Court of the United States and the Negro* (Cleveland: World Publishing Company, 1966), p. 88.

25.   Albert P. Blaustein and Robert L. Zangrando, *Civil Rights and The American Negro: A Documentary* (New York: Trident Press, 1968), pp. 225-26.

26.   U. S., *Constitution,* Amend. XIV.

27.   Logan, *The Negro* I, pp. 24, 44.

28.   U. S., *Constitution,* Amend. XV.

29.   Miller, *The Petitioners,* pp. 96-97; Blaustein and Zangrando, *Civil Rights,* pp. 243-44.

30.   Logan, *The Negro,* I, pp. 31-32.

31.   Miller, *The Petitioners,* pp. 98-99.

32.   George R. Bentley, *A History of the Freedmen's Bureau* (New York: Octagon Books, 1970), pp. 49, 55-56, 76-77, 133.

33.   *Ibid.,* p. 171.

34.   *Ibid.,* p. 172.

35.   *Ibid.,* p. 173; "The Reverend J. S. Nelson to Hannibal D. Norton, Agent, May 24, 1867, Letters Received, Morganton, N. C., Bureau of Refugees, Freedmen and Abandoned Lands," Record Group 105, National Archives, Washington, D.C.

36.   J. W. Alvord, *Schools for Freedmen: 6th Semi-Annual Report, July 1, 1868* (Washington, D.C.: Government Printing Office, 1868), pp. 19, 21.

37.   Alvord, *7th Semi-Annual Report, January 1, 1869,* (1869) pp. 3-7.

38.   *Ibid,* pp. 16-17.

39.   Alvord, *9th Semi-Annual Report, January 1, 1870* (1870) p. 4.

40.   Bentley, *Freedmen's Bureau,* pp. 175-76.

41. Alvord, *9th Semi-Annual Report*, p. 64.

42. Alvord, *7th Semi-Annual Report*, pp. 17, 25-26; *9th Semi-Annual Report*, p. 17.

43. Henry J. Perkinson, *The Imperfect Panacea: American Faith in Education, 1865-1965* (New York: Random House, 1968), pp. 23-25.

44. DuBois, *Black Reconstruction*, pp. 389, 396-97.

45. *Ibid.*, p. 397.

46. *Ibid.*, pp. 651, 653-55.

47. *Ibid.*, pp. 655-56; Edgar Wallace Knight, *The Influence of Reconstruction on Education in the South* (New York: Teachers College, Columbia University, 1913), pp. 32-33.

48. DuBois, *Black Reconstruction*, pp. 656-57; Knight, *Influence of Reconstruction*, p. 21.

49. DuBois, *Black Reconstruction*, pp. .63-65.

50. Henry Allen Bullock, *A History of Negro Education in The South From 1619 to the Present* (New York: Praeger Publishers, 1967), p. 36.

51. *Ibid.*, pp. 47-49, 60, 74-75.

52. Perkinson, *Imperfect Panacea*, pp. 26, 30-31, 34-35.

53. Frank Bowles and Frank A. DeCosta, *Between Two Worlds: A Profile of Negro Higher Education* (New York: McGraw-Hill, 1971), pp. 32-33; H. G. Good, *A History of American Education* (New York: The Macmillan Company, 1962), pp. 299-301.

54. Edgar W. Knight, *Public School Education in North Carolina* (New York: Negro Universities Press, 1969), pp. 297-303.

55. Bowles and DeCosta, *Between Two Worlds*, p. 33.

56. Miller, *The Petitioners*, pp. 102-103.

57. *Ibid.*, pp. 104-107.

58. *Ibid.*, pp. 109-112.

59. *Ibid.*, pp. 112-113.

60. *Ibid.*, pp. 136-37.

61. *Ibid.*, pp. 137-39.

62. Blaustein and Zangrando, *Civil Rights*, p. 276.

63. Paul H. Buck, *The Road to Reunion* (Boston: Little, Brown and Company, 1937), pp. 155-60.

64. *Ibid.*, pp. 147-48, 162, 164; Bullock, *Negro Education*, p. 118.

65. John Hope Franklin, *Reconstruction After The Civil War*

(Chicago: The University of Chicago Press, 1961), pp. 92, 109, 153; Horace Mann Bond, *The Education of The Negro in The American Social Order* (New York: Octagon Books, 1970), pp. 359-60.

66.   Bullock, *Negro Education,* pp. 31-33.

67.   *Ibid.,* p. 76.

68.   Perkinson, *Imperfect Panacea,* p. 28; Merle Curti, *Social Ideas of American Educators* (Paterson, New Jersey: Littlefield, Adams and Company, 1961), p. 263; Bullock, *Negro Education,* p. 57; Knight, *Influence of Reconstruction,* p. 43.

69.   Curti, *Social Ideas,* pp. 263-68.

70.   *Ibid.,* pp. 278-79.

CHAPTER III

1.   Rayford W. Logan, *The Betrayal of the Negro, From Rutherford B. Hayes to Woodrow Wilson* (New York: Collier Books, 1965), pp. 67-70, 195; Merle Curti, *The Social Ideas of American Educators* (Paterson, New Jersey: Littlefield, Adams and Company, 1961), pp. 270-72.

2.   Logan, *The Betrayal,* pp. 70-74.

3.   *Ibid.,* pp. 74-76.

4.   *Ibid.,* p. 85.

5.   *Ibid.,* pp. 199-207.

6.   *Ibid.,* p. 276; Booker T. Washington, *Up From Slavery* (New York: Dell Publishing Company, 1965), pp. 42-55.

7.   *Ibid.,* p. 48; Henry J. Perkinson, *The Imperfect Panacea: American Faith in Education, 1865-1965* (New York: Random House, 1968), p. 43; Walter Fleming, ed., *Documentary History of Reconstruction,* Vol. II (New York: McGraw-Hill Book Company, 1966), pp. 209-10.

8.   Washington, *Up From Slavery,* pp. 56, 60-61, 63, 74-76, 92; Robert L. Factor, *The Black Response to America* (Reading, Massachusetts: Addison-Wesley Publishing Company, 1970), p. 137.

9.   Perkinson, *Imperfect Panacea,* pp. 47-48; Martin E. Dann, ed., *The Black Press, 1827-1890* (New York: Capricorn Books, 1971), p. 356.

10.   August Meier, *Negro Thought in America, 1880-1915* (Ann Arbor: Ann Arbor Paperbacks, 1963), p. 101; Logan, *The Betrayal,* pp. 276-79.

11. Logan, *The Betrayal,* pp. 279-81.

12. *Ibid.,* pp. 83-84, 94, 286.

13. *Ibid.,* pp. 286-87.

14. Albert P. Blaustein and Robert L. Zangrando, *Civil Rights and The American Negro: A Documentary* (New York: Trident Press, 1968), pp. 294-96.

15. David L. Kirp and Mark G. Yudolf, *Educational Policy and The Law* (Berkeley: McCutchan Publishing Corporation, 1974), pp. 281-84.

16. *Ibid.,* p. 285.

17. *Ibid.,* pp. 285-87.

18. Blaustein and Zangrando, *Civil Rights,* pp. 311-12.

19. *Ibid.,* pp. 311-14.

20. Logan, *The Negro,* II, pp. 48, 58-59, 67-68.

21. C. Vann Woodward, *The Strange Career of Jim Crow* (New York: Oxford University Press, 1966), pp. 86-87; Mary F. Berry, *Black Resistance/White Law: A History of Constitutional Racism* (New York: Appleton-Century-Crofts, 1971), p. 124.

22. Blaustein and Zangrando, *Civil Rights,* pp. 314-15.

23. Alfred H. Kelly and Winfred A. Harbison, *The American Constitution: Its Origin and Development* (New York: W. W. Norton and Company, 1963), p. 492.

24. Elisabeth S. Peck, *Berea's First Century, 1855-1955* (Lexington, Kentucky: University of Kentucky Press, 1955), pp. 49-53; David Nelson, "Experiment in Interracial Education at Berea College, 1858-1908," *Journal of Negro History* LIX (January, 1974), pp. 13-27.

25. Meier, *Negro Thought,* p. 22.

26. *Ibid.*

27. *Ibid.,* pp. 22-24.

28. Henry Allen Bullock, *A History of Negro Education in The South From 1619 to the Present* (New York: Praeger Publishers, 1967), p. 77.

29. H. G. Good, *A History of American Education* (New York: The Macmillan Company, 1962), pp. 299-301.

30. Bullock, *Negro Education,* pp. 86-87.

31. Frank Bowles and Frank A. DeCosta, *Between Two Worlds: A Profile of Negro Higher Education* (New York: McGraw-Hill, 1971), pp. 38-39.

32. Bullock, *Negro Education,* p. 148.

140 *The Lengthening Shadow of Slavery*

33. *Ibid.*, pp. 129-31, 158.
34. *Ibid.*, pp. 84-85.
35. Lewis James, "The Agent as a Factor in the Education of Negroes in the South," *Journal of Negro Education* XIX (Winter, 1950), pp. 31-33, 34, 36, 37.
36. Arthur D. Wright, *Negro School Fund, Inc.* (Washington, D.C.: The Negro Rural School Fund, Inc., 1933), pp. iii, 11.
37. Thomas J. Jones, *Educational Adaptations: Report of Ten Years' Work of the Phelps-Stokes Fund, 1910-1920* (New York: Phelps-Stokes Fund, 1920), p. 69.
38. Bullock, *Negro Education,* pp. 126-27; Meier, *Negro Thought,* p. 133.
39. W. E. B. DuBois, *The Education of Black People: Ten Critiques, 1906-1960,* edited by Herbert Aptheker, (Amherst: The University of Massachusetts Press, 1973), pp. 17-18.
40. Perkinson, *Imperfect Panacea,* p. 29.
41. Bullock, *Negro Education,* pp. 16-67.
42. *Ibid.*, pp. 185-86.
43. *Ibid.*, p. 194.
44. W. E. B. DuBois, *Dusk of Dawn,* (New York: Schocken Books, 1968), pp. 25, 47.
45. W. E. B. DuBois, *The Suppression of the African Slave Trade to the United States of America, 1638-1870* (New York: Dover Publications 1970), p. vi; Kelly Miller, *Radicals and Conservatives* (New York: Schocken Books, 1968), p. 29.
46. W. E. B. DuBois, *The Philadelphia Negro* (New York: Schocken Books, 1967), pp. ix-xliv.
47. Logan, *The Betrayal,* p. 329; John H. Bracey, Jr., et al., *Black Sociologists: The First Half Century* (Belmont, California: Wadsworth Publishing Company), p. 3; Allen B. Ballard, *Education of Black Folk* (New York: Harper Colophon Books, 1973), p. 19.
48. Bracey, *Black Sociologists,* p. 18.
49. *Ibid.*, p. 27.
50. W. E. B. DuBois, *Souls of Black Folk* (New York: New American Library, Inc., 1969),pp. 79-80; Robert H. Brisbane, *Black Vanguard* (Valley Forge, Pennsylvania: Judson Press, 1970), p. 39.
51. DuBois, *Souls of Black Folks,* pp. 86-87.
52. *Ibid.*, pp. 88-89.
53. *Ibid.*, pp. 89-90.

54. *Ibid.*, pp. 93-94.
55. John Hope Franklin and Isidore Starr, eds., *The Negro in Twentieth Century America* (New York: Vintage Books, 1967), p. 265.
56. *Ibid.*, p. 267.
57. *Ibid.*, pp. 268-69.
58. *Ibid.*, p. 270.
59. *Ibid.*, p. 271.
60. *Ibid.*, pp. 274-75.
61. Robert L. Factor, *Black Response to America* (Reading, Massachusetts: Addison-Wesley Publishing Co., 1970), pp. 255-57; Leslie H. Fishel and Benjamin Quarles, *The Black American: A Documentary History* (Glenview, Illinois: Scott Foresmen and Company, 1970), pp. 350-51.
62. Factor, *Black Response,* p. 260.
63. *Ibid.*, pp. 261-62.
64. *Ibid.*, pp. 272-277.
65. *Ibid.*, pp. 285-286; Meier, *Negro Thought,* pp. 176-177.
66. Meier, *Negro Thought,* p. 177; Edward Peeks, *The Long Struggle for Black Power* (New York: Charles Scribner's Sons, 1971), p. 143.
67. Meier, *Negro Thought,* p. 177.
68. *Ibid.*, p. 178; Herbert Aptheker, ed., *Documentary History of the Negro People in the United States,* Vol. II (New York: The Citadel Press, 1964), pp. 900-901.
69. Aptheker, *Documentary History,* II, pp. 901-904; Meier, *Negro Thought,* p. 178.
70. Aptheker, *Documentary History,* II, pp. 907-910; Logan, *The Negro,* pp. 63-64.
71. Meier, *Negro Thought,* pp. 179-181.
72. *Ibid.*, pp. 182-183.
73. Booker T. Washington and W. E. B. DuBois, *The Negro in the South* (New York: Citadel Press, 1970), pp. i, 102-103.
74. Aptheker, *Documentary History,* II, p. 883.
75. Perkinson, *Imperfect Panacea,* p. 55.
76. David B. Tyack, ed., *Turning Point in American Educational History* (Lexington, Mass.: Xerox Publishing Corporation, 1967), p. 298; W. E. B. DuBois, *The ABC of Color* (New York: International Publishers, 1963), p. 33; Washington, *Up From Slavery,* p. 219.
77. David Loye, *The Healing of a Nation,* (New York: Dell

Publishing Company, 1971), p. 213; DuBois, *ABC of Color,* p. 20.
    78.   Loye, *The Healing,* pp. 213-14.
    79.   Ballard, *The Education,* pp. 18-19; S. P. Fullinwider, *The Mind and Mood of Black America* (Homewood, Illinois: Dorsey Press, 1969), pp. 66-67.
    80.   See the first volume of Louis R. Harlan's *Booker T. Washington: The Making of a Black Leader, 1856-1901* (New York: Oxford University Press, 1972).

CHAPTER IV

    1.   Albert P. Blaustein and Robert L. Zangrando, *Civil Rights and The American Negro: A Documentary History* (New York: Trident Press, 1968), pp. 330-38, 388.
    2.   Emmett J. Scott, *Negro Migration During The War* (New York: Arno Press and *The New York Times,* 1969), pp. 18, 22.
    3.   *Ibid.,* p. 14, Louis V. Kennedy, *The Negro Peasant Turns Cityward* (New York: Columbia University Press, 1930), pp. 44-46.
    4.   Scott, *Negro Migration,* pp. 30-31.
    5.   *Ibid.,* p. 50.
    6.   *Ibid.,* p. 17.
    7.   August Meier and Elliott Rudwick, *From Plantation to Ghetto: An Interpretive History of American Negroes* (New York: Hill and Wang, Inc., 1966), p. 197.
    8.   Benjamin Quarles, *The Negro in The Making of America* (New York: Collier Books, 1964), p. 182.
    9.   *Ibid.,* p. 189.
    10.   Rayford W. Logan, *The Negro in The United States,* Vol. I (New York: Van Nostrand, Reinhold Company, 1970), pp. 79-80; Meier and Rudwick, *From Plantation,* p. 194.
    11.   Virgil A. Clift et al., eds., *Negro Education in America: Its Adequacy, Problems, and Needs* (New York: Harper and Brothers, 1962), pp. 52-53.
    12.   Doxey A. Wilkinson, *Special Problems of Negro Education* (Westport, Connecticut: Negro Universities Press, 1970), p. 59.
    13.   Dwight C. W. Holmes, *The Evaluation of The Negro College* (New York: Arno Press and *The New York Times,* 1969), p. 150.
    14.   *Ibid.,* p. 159.
    15.   *Ibid.,* pp. 158, 161.

16.   Harry Washington Greene, *Holders of Doctorates Among American Negroes* (Boston: Meador Publishing Company, 1946), p. 26. An extremely useful book, but not entirely accurate. At least one white doctorate was included.

17.   Thomas Jesse Jones, ed., *Negro Education: A Study of the Private and Higher Schools for Colored People in the United States,* Vol. II (New York: Arno Press and *The New York Times,* 1969), p. 17.

18.   Robert H. Brisbane, *Black Vanguard* (Valley Forge, Pennsylvania: Judson Press, 1970), p. 102; Rayford W. Logan, *Howard University: The First Hundred Years, 1867-1967* (New York: New York University Press, 1968), pp. 231-44.

19.   Herbert Aptheker, *Afro-American History: The Modern Era* (Secaucus, New Jersey: The Citadel press, 1973), pp. 178-79.

20.   *Ibid.,* pp. 183-84.

21.   Holmes, *Negro College,* pp. 184-85.

22.   *Ibid.,* p. 170; *Proceedings and Reports of the John F. Slater Fund to the Year Ending June 30, 1932,* p. 10.

23.   Holmes, *Negro College,* pp. 184-85.

24.   Rufus F. Clement, "The Historical Development of Higher Education for Negro Americans," *Journal of Negro Education* XXXV (Fall, 1966), pp. 302-303.

25.   *Ibid.,* p. 302.

26.   Wilkerson, *Special Problems,* pp. 65, 151-52.

27.   W. E. B. DuBois, *The Education of Black People: Ten Critiques, 1906-1960,* Herbert Aptheker, ed. (Amherst: The University of Massachusetts Press, 1973), pp. 65, 92, 146-47; Irvin V. Shannon, *Negro Education and The Development of a Group Tradition* (Nashville: A Condensation of a Thesis in Sociology, Vanderbilt University, 1934), pp. 3, 6.

28.   Horace Mann Bond, "The Education and Present Status of Negro Higher and Professional Education in The United States," *Journal of Negro Education* XVII, (Summer, 1948), p. 224.

29.   Greene, *Holders of Doctorates,* pp. 23-24.

30.   Holmes, *Negro College,* p. 190.

31.   George N. Redd, "The Educational and Cultural Level of the American Negro," *Journal of Negro Education* XIX (Summer, 1950), p. 250; Leander L. Boykin, "The Status and Trends of Differentials Between White and Negro Teachers' Salaries in the Southern States, 1900-1946," *Journal of Negro Education* XVIII (Winter, 1949), p. 41.

32.   Charles Johnson, et al., *The Collapse of Cotton Tenancy* (Chapel Hill: The University of North Carolina Press, 1935), pp. 4-5, 14, 16-17.

33.   *Ibid.*, pp. 48-50.

34.   Bullock, *Negro Education*, p. 190; Meier and Rudwick, *From Plantation*, pp. 211-12; Logan, *The Negro*, I, pp. 86-89.

35.   John Hope Franklin, *From Slavery to Freedom: A History of Negro Americans*, 3rd edition (New York: Alfred A. Knopf, 1967), p. 576.

36.   *Ibid.*, pp. 576-77.

37.   *Ibid.*, pp. 577-78.

38.   Quarles, *Negro In America*, p. 217.

39.   Executive Order 8802, June 25, 1941, 6 *Federal Register* 3109 (1941).

40.   Quarles, *Negro In America*, p. 217.

41.   Franklin, *From Slavery*, pp. 592-96.

42.   *Ibid.*, pp. 584-85; Logan, *The Negro*, I, pp. 98-101; Rayford W. Logan, "The Evolution of Private Colleges for Negroes," *Journal of Negro Education* XXVII (Summer, 1958), pp. 219-20.

43.   Ambrose Caliver, *Postwar Education of Negroes* (Washington, D.C.: U. S. Office of Education, 1945), p. 35.

44.   *Ibid.*, p. 48.

45.   National Association for the Advancement of Colored People, *G. I. Bill of Rights: A Guide* (New York: NAACP, 1952), p. 13.

46.   Frank Bowles and Frank A. DeCosta, *Between Two Worlds: A Profile of Negro Higher Education* (New York: McGraw-Hill, 1971), pp. 52-53.

47.   Rayford W. Logan and Michael Winston, *The Negro in The United States*, Vol. II (New York: Van Nostrand Reinhold Company, 1971), pp. 43, 111-12.

48.   Wilkerson, *Special Problems*, pp. 60, 66; In 1927, in the case of *Gong Lum* v. *Rice*, The Supreme Court upheld for the last time a segregation law or any other type of racial classification. Here the case involved classifying an Asian American as colored and requiring her to attend the colored school since there were no schools in Mississippi for persons of Chinese extraction; Blaustein and Zangrando, *Civil Rights*, pp. 406-7.

49.   Bullock, *Negro Education*, p. 227.

50.   Blaustein and Zangrando, *Civil Rights*, pp. 407-10; Loren

Miler, *The Petitioners: The Story of the Supreme Court of the United States and the Negro* (Cleveland: World Publishing Company, 1966), pp. 333-34.

51. Miller, *The Petitioners*, p. 335.
52. *Ibid.,* pp. 338-40.
53. *Ibid.,* pp. 336-37.
54. Bullock, *Negro Education*, pp. 230-31.

CHAPTER V

1. Henry Allen Bullock, *A History of Negro Education in the South From 1619 to the Present* (New York: Praeger Publishers, 1967), p. 231.
2. *Ibid.,* pp. 231-32.
3. *Ibid.,* p. 233.
4. Albert P. Blaustein and Robert L. Zangrando, *Civil Rights and the American Negro: A Documentary History* (New York: Trident Press, 1968), pp. 414-17.
5. Loren Miller, *The Petitioners: The Story of The Supreme Court of the United States and the Negro* (Cleveland: World Publishing Company, 1966), pp. 349-51.
6. Benjamin Muse, *Ten Years of Prelude: The Story of Integration Since the Supreme Court's 1954 Decision* (New York: Viking Press, 1964), pp. 67-72.
7. *Ibid.,* pp. 146-59.
8. See Hodding Carter, *The South Strikes Back* (Garden City, New Jersey: Doubleday, 1959), which is a case study of the White Citizens' Council in Mississippi.
9. Blaustein and Zangrando, *Civil Rights*, pp. 451-53.
10. *Ibid.,* p. 465; Miller, *The Petitioners*, pp. 356-58.
11. 377 U. S. 218 (1964).
12. 391. U. S. 430 (1968).
13. 402 U. S. 1 (1971).
14. *Ibid.,* p. 30.
15. *Ibid.,* p. 43.
16. *Ibid.,* p. 46.
17. *Ibid.,* p. 33.
18. *Ibid.,* p. 26.
19. Frank Goodman, "De Facto School Segregation: A

Constitutional and Empirical Analysis," 60 *California Law Review*, 275 (1972), pp. 285-286.

20.   413 U. S. 186 (1973).
21.   *Ibid.*, p. 189.
22.   93 S. Ct. 2701.
23.   94 S. Ct. 3112 (1974).
24.   490 F. 2d 1154 (1974).
25.   *Ibid.*, p. 1157.
26.   480 F. 2d 1159 (1973).
27.   *Ibid.*, pp. 20-21.
28.   356 F. Supp. 1227 (1973).
29.   *Ibid.*, p. 1238.
30.   Herbert O. Reid, Sr., "Twenty Year Assessment of School Desegregation," 19 *Howard Law Journal* (Winter, 1975), pp. 18-19.
31.   416 U. S. 312 (1974).
32.   Brief for Respondents as *Amicus Curiae* at 11, *DeFunis* v. *Odegaard*, 416 U. S. 312 (1974).
33.   K. S. Tollett, "The Role of the Law Center in Urban Society," A Paper presented at the dedication of the Charles Klein Law Building, Temple University, Philadelphia, Pennsylvania, April 17, 1975.
34.   Martin Luther King, Jr., *Stride Toward Freedom* (New York: Harper and Brothers, 1958), pp. 43, 71-89, 108-188, 216-224.
35.   Howard Zinn, *SNCC: Student Nonviolent Coordinating Committee: The New Abolitionists* (Boston: The Beacon Press, 1965), pp. 1-40.
36.   Jack Mendelsohn, *The Martyrs: Sixteen Who Gave Their Lives For Racial Justice* (New York: Harper and Row Publishing Co., 1971), pp. 109-32.
37.   Rayford W. Logan and Michael Winston, *The Negro in the United States, Volume II: The Ordeal of Democracy* (New York: Van Nostrand Reinhold Company, 1971), pp. 20-21.
38.   The previous day W. E. B. DuBois died in Ghana where he renounced his American citizenship. DuBois had been one of America's most persistent social critics. *Ibid.*, p. 26.
39.   *The New York Times*, August 29, 1963, p. 21.
40.   *Ibid.*, p. 26.
41.   Blaustein and Zangrando, *Civil Rights*, pp. 472-84.
42.   Logan and Winston, *The Negro*, II, pp. 24-25, 143-45.

43. Blaustein and Zangrando, *Civil Rights,* pp. 526-50.

44. *Ibid.,* pp. 523-24, 551.

45. *Ibid.,* pp. 566-72.

46. Logan and Winston, *The Negro,* II, 29-30.

47. *Ibid.,* p. 60.

48. *Equal Employment Opportunity Act,* 42 U. S. C.A. 2000.

49. United States Commission on Civil Rights, *The Federal Civil Rights Enforcement Effort* (Washington, D. C.: U. S. Government Printing Office, 1971), p. xv.

50. United States Commission on Civil Rights, *The Federal Civil Rights Enforcement Effort—A Reassessment* (Washington, D.C.: U. S. Government Printing Office, 1973), pp. 1, 4-5.

51. *Ibid.,* pp. 9-11.

52. *Report of The National Advisory Commission on Civil Disorders* (Washington, D.C.: U. S. Government Printing Office, 1968.), p. 1.

53. *Ibid.,* p. 5.

54. *Ibid.,* p. 5.

55. *Ibid.,* pp. 6-7.

56. *Ibid.,* p. 7.

57. *Ibid.,* pp. 11-12.

58. United States Department of Commerce, Census Bureau, *Social and Economic Characteristics of the Black Population, 1974,* Series p. 23, No. 54, pp. 2, 30-33.

59. National Urban League Research Department, *Quarterly Economic Report on the Black Worker,* Report No. 2 (May, 1975), p. 1.

60. *Ibid.*

61. *Ibid.,* pp. 1-2.

62. *Ibid.,* p. 2.

63. *Ibid.,* p. 5.

64. The Potomac Institute, *Affirmative Action: The Unrealized Goal* (Washington, D.C.: The Potomac Institute, 1973), p. 5.

65. *Ibid.,* pp. 5-6.

66. *Ibid.,* pp. 7-8.

67. *Ibid.,* pp. 8-9; United States Department of Health, Education and Welfare, *Higher Education Guidelines, Executive Order 11246* (Washington, D.C.: U. S. Government Printing Office, 1973), pp. 1-4.

68. HEW, *Guidelines,* pp. 3-4.

69.   U.S.C.C.R. *Federal Civil Rights Enforcement Effort–1974: To Ensure Equal Educational Opportunity* (Washington, D.C.; U. S. Government Printing Office, 1975), p. 195.

70.   U. S. Census, *Social and Economic Characteristics of the Black Population,* p. 94; See the Institute for the Study of Educational Policy's *Equal Educational Opportunity for Blacks in U. S. Higher Education: An Assessment* (To be published by Howard University Press, Washington, D.C., in 1976) for a detailed discussion of the barriers to access, distribution, and enrollment.

71.   Institute for the Study of Educational Policy, *The Status of Affirmative Action for Blacks in Higher Education* (A Report to be published by Howard University Press, Washington, D.C. in 1976).

72.   *Ibid.*

BIBLIOGRAPHY

Alvord, J. W. *Schools for Freedmen: Ninth Semi-Annual Report,* January 1, 1870. Washington, D. C.: Government Printing Office, 1870.

———. *Schools for Freedmen: Seventh Semi-Annual Report,* January 1, 1869. Washington, D. C.: Government Printing Office, 1869.

———. *Schools for Freedmen: Sixth Semi-Annual Report,* July 1, 1868. Washington, D. C.: Government Printing Office, 1868.

Amherst Alumni News. Winter 1962.

Andrews, Sidney. *The South Since the War.* Boston: Tickner and Fields, 1866.

Aptheker, Herbert. *Afro-American History: The Modern Era.* Secaucus, New Jersey: The Citadel Press, 1973.

———. *American Negro Slave Revolts.* New York: International Publishers, 1969.

———. ed., *Documentary History of the Negro People in The United States.* Vol. II. New York: The Citadel Press, 1964.

Ballard, Allen B. *Education of Black Folk.* New York: Harper Colophon Books, 1973.

Bentley, George R. *A History of The Freedmen's Bureau.* New York: Octagon Books, 1970.

Berry, Mary F. *Black Resistance/White Law: A History of Constitutional Racism.* New York: Appleton-Century-Crofts, 1971.

Blassingame, John W. *The Slave Community: Plantation Life in The Ante-Bellum South.* New York: Oxford University Press, 1972.

Blaustein, Albert P. and Robert L. Zangrando. *Civil Rights and the American Negro: A Documentary History.* New York: Trident Press, 1968.

Bond, Horace Mann. *The Education of the Negro in the American Social Order.* New York: Octagon Books, 1970.

———. "The Evaluation and Present Status of Negro Higher and Professional Education in the United States," *Journal of Negro Education* XXVII (Summer, 1948).

Bowles, Frank and Frank A. DeCosta. *Between Two Worlds: A Profile of Negro Higher Education.* New York: McGraw-Hill, 1971.

Boykin, Leander L. "The Status and Trends of Differentials Between White and Negro Teachers' Salaries in the Southern States, 1900-1946," *Journal of Negro Education* XVII (Winter, 1949).

Bracey, John H. et al. *Black Sociologists: The First Half Century.* Belmont, California: Wadsworth Publishing Company, 1971.

Brawley, Benjamin. *A Social History of the American Negro.* New York: Collier Books, 1970.

Brisbane, Robert. *Black Vanguard.* Valley Forge, Pennsylvania: Judson Press, 1970.

Brooks, Albert N. D. "Education of the Negro in Virginia Prior to 1861." Washington, D. C.: Unpublished Master of Arts Thesis, 1938.

Buck, Paul H. *The Road to Reunion.* Boston: Little, Brown and Company 1937.

Bullock, Henry Allen. *A History of Negro Education in the South From 1619 to the Present.* New York: Praeger Publishers, 1967.

Burgess, John W. *Reconstruction and the Constitution, 1866-1876.* New York: Charles Scribner's Sons, 1907.

Caliver, Ambrose. *Postwar Education of Negroes.* Washington, D. C.: U. S. Office of Education, 1945.

Carter, Hodding. *The South Strikes Back.* Garden City, New Jersey: Doubleday, 1959.

The Charleston Daily Courier. September, November, 1865.

Clement, Rufus F. "The Historical Development of Higher Education for Negro Americans," *Journal of Negro Education* XXXV (Fall, 1966).

Clift, Virgil A. et al., eds. *Negro Education in America: Its Adequacy, Problems and Needs.* New York: Harper and Brothers, 1962.

Cox, LaWanda and John H. Cox, *Politics, Principles and Prejudice, 1865 1866: Dilemma of Reconstruction America*. New York: Atheneum Press, 1969.

Curti, Merle, *Social Ideas of American Educators*. Paterson, New Jersey: Littlefield, Adams and Company, 1961.

Draper, Theodore. *The Rediscovery of Black Nationalism*. New York: The Viking Press, 1969.

DuBois, W. E. B. *The ABC of Color*. New York: International Publishers, 1963.

————. *Black Reconstruction in America, 1860-1880*. Cleveland: Meridian Books, 1964.

————. *Dusk of Dawn*. New York: Schocken Books, 1968.

————. *The Education of Black People: Ten Critiques, 1906-1960*. Herbert Aptheker, ed. Amherst: The University of Massachusetts Press, 1973.

————. ed. *Negro Artisan*. New York: Arno Press and *The New York Times*, 1969.

————. *The Philadelphia Negro*. New York: Schocken Books, 1967.

————. *Souls of Black Folk*. New York: New American Library, Inc., 1969.

————. *The Suppression of The African Slave Trade to the United States of America, 1638-1870*. New York: Dover Publications, Inc., 1967.

"Eighteenth Century Petition of South Carolina Negroes," *Journal of Negro History* XXXI (1946), 98-99.

Equal Employment Opportunity Act, 42 U. S. C. A. 2000e.

Executive Order 8802, June 25, 1941. 6 *Federal Register*. 3109 (1941).

Factor, Robert L. *Black Response to America*. Reading, Massachusetts: Addison-Wesley Publishing Company, 1970.

Farnam, Henry W. *Chapters in the History of Social Legislation in the United States to 1860*. Washington, D. C.: Carnegie Institution of Washington, 1938.

Feldstein, Stanley. *Once a Slave: The Slave's View of Slavery*. New York: William Morrow and Company, Inc., 1971.

Fishel, Leslie H., Jr. and Benjamin Quarles. *The Black American: A Documentary History*. Glenview, Illinois: Scott, Foresman and Company, 1970.

Fite, Gilbert C. and Jim C. Reese. *An Economic History of the United States*. Boston: Houghton Mifflin, 1965.

Fleming, Walter L. *Documentary History of Reconstruction*. 2 volumes. Cleveland: The Arthur H. Clark Company, 1906.

Franklin, John Hope. *The Emancipation Proclamation*. Garden City, New

Jersey: Anchor Books, 1965.

————. *From Slavery to Freedom: A History of Negro Americans*. 3rd edition. New York: Alfred A. Knopf, 1967.

———— and Isidore Starr, eds. *The Negro in Twentieth Century America*. New York: Vintage Books, 1967.

————. *Reconstruction After the Civil War*. Chicago: The University of Chicago Press, 1961.

Franklin, Raymond S. and Solomon Resnik. *The Political Economy of Racism*. New York: Holt, Rinehart and Winston, 1973.

Fullinwider, S. P. *The Mind and Mood of Black America*. Homewood, Illinois: Dorsey Press, 1969.

Genovese, Eugene, ed. *The Slave Economics*. Vol. II. New York: John Wiley and Sons, Inc., 1973.

Good, H. G. *A History of American Education*. New York: The Macmillan Company, 1962.

Goodell, William. *The American Slave Code in Theory and in Practice*. London: Clarke, Beeton and Company, 1853.

Goodman, Frank. "De Facto School Segregation: A Constitutional and Empirical Analysis," 60 *California Law Review* 275 (1972).

Greene, Harry Washington. *Holders of Doctorates Among American Negroes*. Boston: Meador Publishing Company, 1946.

Greene, Lorenzo J. *The Negro in Colonial New England, 1620-1776*. New York: Columbia University Press, 1942.

Grimke, John F., Compiler. *The Public Laws of the State of South Carolina From Its First Establishment as a British Province Down to the Year 1790*. Philadelphia: R. Aitken and Sons, 1790.

Hacker, Louis M. *The Triumph of American Capitalism*. New York: Simon and Schuster, 1940.

Harlan, Louis R. *Booker T. Washington: The Making of a Black Leader, 1856-1902*. New York: Oxford University Press, 1972.

Holmes, Dwight C. W. *The Evaluation of the Negro College*. New York: Arno Press and *The New York Times*, 1969.

Hopkins, Vincent C. *Dred Scott's Case*. New York: Fordham University Press, 1951.

Hurd, John C. *The Law of Freedom and Bondage in the United States*. 2 Volumes. New York: Negro Universities Press, 1968.

Institute for the Study of Educational Policy. *Equal Educational Opportunity for Blacks in U.S. Higher Education: An Assessment*. Washington, D.C.: Howard University Press, 1976.

Institute for the Study of Educational Policy. *The Status of Affirmative Action for Blacks in Higher Education*. A Report to be published by Howard University Press, Washington, D. C., in 1976.

"The Iron-Willed Black Schoolmaster and his Granite Academy." *Middlebury College NewsLetter*. (Spring, 1974). pp. 6-14.

James, Lewis. "The Agent as a Factor in the Education of Negroes in the South," *Journal of Negro Education* xix (Winter, 1950).

Jenkins, William Sumner. *Pro-Slavery Thought in the Old South*. Gloucester, Massachusetts: Peter Smith, 1960.

The John F. Slater Fund, *Proceeding and Reports to the Year Ending June 30, 1932*.

Johnson, Charles, et al., *The Collapse of Cotton Tenancy*. Chapel Hill: The University of North Carolina Press, 1935.

Johnson, Guion G. *Ante-Bellum North Carolina: A Social History*. Chapel Hill: The University of North Carolina Press, 1937.

Jones, Thomas J. *Educational Adaptations: Report of Ten Years Work of The Phelps-Stokes Fund, 1910-1920*. New York: Phelps-Stokes Fund, 1920.

Jones, Thomas Jesse, ed. *Negro Education: A Study of the Private and Higher Schools for Colored people in the United States*. Vol. II. New York: Arno Press and *The New York Times*, 1969.

Jordan, Winthrop. *White Over Black: American Attitudes Toward the Negro, 1550-1812*. Baltimore: Penguin Books, Inc., 1969.

Kelly, Alfred H. and Winfred A. Harbison. *The American Constitution: Its Origins and Development*. New York: W. W. Norton and Company, 1963.

Kennedy, Louis V. *The Negro Peasant Turns Cityward*. New York: Columbia University Press, 1930.

King, Martin Luther, Jr. *Stride Toward Freedom*. New York: Harper and Brothers, 1958.

Kirp, David L. and Mark G. Yudof. *Educational Policy and the Law*. Berkeley: McCutchan Publishing Corporation, 1974.

Knight, Edgar Wallace. *The Influence of Reconstruction on Education in the South*. New York: Teachers College, Columbia University, 1913.

————. *Public School Education in North Carolina*. New York: Negro Universities Press, 1969.

Letters Received, Bureau of Refugees, Freedmen and Abandoned Lands, Record Group 105, National Archives, Washington, D. C.

Litwack, Leon F. *North of Slavery: The Negro in the Free States, 1790-1860*. Chicago: The University of Chicago Press, 1961.

Lofton, John. *Insurrection in South Carolina*. Yellow Springs, Ohio: Antioch Press, 1964.

Logan, Rayford W. and Michael Winston. *The Negro in the United States, Volume II: The Ordeal of Democracy*. New York: Van Nostrand Reinhold Company, 1971.

Logan, Rayford W. *The Betrayal of the Negro: From Rutherford B. Hayes to Woodrow Wilson*. New York: Collier Books, 1965.

———. *Howard University: The First Hundred Years, 1867-1967*. New York: New York University Press, 1968.

———. "The Evolution of Private Colleges for Negroes," *Journal of Negro Education* XXVII (Summer, 1953).

———. *The Negro in the United States, Volume I: A History to 1945—From Slavery to Second-class Citizenship*. New York: Van Nostrand Reinhold Company, 1970.

Loye, David. *The Healing of a Nation*. New York: Dell Publishing Company, 1971.

McKitrick, Eric L., ed. *Slavery Defended: The Views of the Old South*. Englewood Cliffs, New Jersey: Prentice Hall, 1963.

McManus, Edgar J. *A History of Negro Slavery in New York*. Syracuse: Syracuse University Press, 1966.

Meier, August and Elliott Rudwick. *From Plantation to Ghetto: An Interpretive History of American Negroes*. New York: Hill and Wang, Inc., 1966.

———. *Negro Thought in America, 1880-1915*. Ann Arbor: Ann Arbor Paperbacks, 1963.

Mendelsohn, Jack. *The Martyrs: Sixteen Who Gave Their Lives for Racial Justice*. New York: Harper and Row Publishing Company, 1971.

Miller, Kelly. *Radicals and Conservatives*. New York: Schocken Books, 1968.

Miller, Loren. *The Petitioners: The Story of the Supreme Court of the United States and the Negro*. Cleveland: World Publishing Company, 1966.

Muse, Benjamin. *Ten Years of Prelude: The Story of Integration Since The Supreme Court's 1954 Decision*. New York: Viking, 1964.

National Association for the Advancement of Colored People. *G. I. Bill of Rights: A Guide*. New York: National Association for the Advancement of Colored People, 1952.

National Urban League Research Department, *Quarterly Economic Report on the Black Worker*, Report No. 2. May, 1975.

Nelson, Paul David. "Experiment in Interracial Education at Berea College,

1858-1908," *Journal of Negro History* LIX (January, 1974), 13-27.

New York Times, August 29, 1963.

North, Douglas. *The Economic Growth of the United States, 1790-1860.* Englewood Cliffs, New Jersey: Prentice-Hall, 1961.

Peck, Elisabeth S. *Berea's First Century, 1855-1955.* Lexington: University of Kentucky Press, 1955.

Peeks, Edward. *The Long Struggle for Black Power.* New York: Charles Scribner's Sons, 1971.

Perkinson, Henry J. *The Imperfect Panacea: American Faith in Education, 1865-1965.* New York: Random House, 1968.

The Potomac Institute. *Affirmative Action: The Unrealized Goal.* Washington, D. C.: The Potomac Institute, Inc., 1973.

Quarles, Benjamin. *Black Abolitionists.* London: Oxford University Press, 1969.

————. *The Negro in the American Revolution.* Chapel Hill: University of North Carolina Press, 1961.

————. *The Negro in the Making of America.* New York: Collier Books. 1964.

Redd, George N. "The Educational and Cultural Level of the American Negro," *Journal of Negro Education* XIX (Summer, 1950).

Reid, Herbert O., Sr. "Twenty Year Assessment of School Desegregation," 19 *Harvard Law Journal* (Winter, 1975).

Report of the National Advisory Commission on Civil Disorders, Washington, D. C.: U. S. Government Printing Office, 1968.

Reports and Resolutions of the South Carolina General Assembly, 1865-1866. Columbia, South Carolina: State Printing Office, n.d.

Reynolds, John S. *Reconstruction in South Carolina.* Columbia, South Carolina: The State Company, 1905.

Richardson, James D., ed. *A Compilation of the Messages and Papers of the Presidents.* Vol. VI. Washington, D. C.: Government Printing Office, 1897.

Rogers, Joel A. *Africa's Gift to America.* New York: Helga M. Rogers, 1961.

Rozwenc, Edwin C., ed. *The Causes of the American Civil War.* Lexington, Massachusetts: D. C. Heath and Company, 1972.

Schurz, Carl. *The Reminiscences of Carl Schurz.* Vol. III. New York: McClure Company, 1908.

Scott, Emmett J. *Negro Migration During the War.* New York: Arno Press and *The New York Times,* 1969.

Shannon, Irvin V. *Negro Education and the Development of a Group Tradi-*

tion. Nashville: A Condensation of a Thesis in Sociology, Vanderbilt University, 1934.

Simkins Francis B. and Robert H. Woody. *South Carolina During Reconstruction*. Chapel Hill: The University of North Carolina Press, 1932.

Spero, Sterling D. and Abram L. Harris. *The Black Worker*. New York: Atheneum, 1972.

Stampp, Kenneth M. *The Peculiar Institution: Slavery in the Ante-Bellum South*. New York: Vintage Books, 1956.

Sydnor, Charles S. *Slavery in Mississippi*. Baton Rouge: Louisiana State University Press, 1966.

Tollett, Kenneth S. "The Role of the Law Center in Urban Society. "A paper presented at the dedication of the Charles Klein Law Building, Temple University, Philadelphia, Penssylvania, April 17, 1975.

Trelease, Allen W. *White Terror, The Ku Klux Conspiracy and Southern Reconstruction*. New York: Harper and Row, 1971.

Trowbridge, John T. *The Desolate South, 1865-1866*. Gordan Carroll, ed. New York: Duell, Sloan and Pearce, 1956.

————. *The South: A Journey Through the Desolated States And Talks With the People*. Hartford, Connecticut: L. Stebbins, 1866.

Tyack, David B., ed. *Turning Points in American Educational History*. Lexington, Massachusetts: Xerox Publishing Corporation, 1967.

U. S. Constitution.

United States Commission on Civil Rights. *The Federal Civil Rights Enforcement Effort*, Washington, D. C.: U. S. Government Printing Office, 1971.

————. *The Federal Civil Rights Enforcement Effort–A Reassessment*. Washington, D. C.: U. S. Government Printing Office, 1973.

————. *Federal Civil Rights Enforcement Effort–1974 To Ensure Equal Educational Opportunity*. U. S. Government Printing Office, 1975.

United States Department of Commerce, Census Bureau. *Social And Economic Characterics of the Black Population, 1974*, Series p. 23. No. 54.

United States Department Of Health, Education And Welfare. *Higher Education Guidelines: Executive Order 11246*. U.S. Government Printing Office, 1973.

Van Noppen, Ira. *The South: A Documentary History*. Princeton, New Jersey: D. Van Nostrand Company, Inc., 1958.

Washington, Booker T. and W. E. B. DuBois. *The Negro In The South*. New York: Citadel Press, 1970.

Washington, Booker T. *Up From Slavery*. New York: Dell Publishing Company, 1965.

Wesley, Charles H. *Negro Labor In The United States*. New York: Russell and Russell, 1967.

Wilbur, Henry W. *President Lincoln's Attitude Toward Slavery and Emancipation*. New York: Bible And Tanner, 1970.

Wilkinson, Doxey A. *Special Problems of Negro Education*. Westport, Connecticut: Negro Universities Press, 1970.

Williams, Eric. *Capitalism And Slavery*. Chapel Hill: University Of North Carolina Press, 1944.

Williamson, Joel. *After Slavery: The Negro In South Carolina During Reconstruction, 1861-1877*. Chapel Hill: The University of North Carolina Press, 1965.

Wilson, Henry. *The Rise And Fall of the Slave Power in America*. Vol. III. Boston: James R. Osgood and Company, 1877.

Wilson, Theodore B. *The Black Codes of the South*. University, Alabama: University of Alabama Press, 1965.

Wiltse, Charles M., ed. *David Walker's Appeal to the Colored Citizens of the World*. New York: Hill And Wang, Inc., 1965.

Woodman, Harold D., ed. *Slavery and the Southern Economy*. New York: Harcourt, Brace and World, 1966.

Woodson, Carter G. *The Education of the Negro Prior to 1861*. New York: Arno Press and *The New York Times*, 1968.

————. *Negro Orators and Their Orations*. Washington, D. C.: Associated Publishers, 1925.

Woodward, C. Vann. *The Strange Career of Jim Crow*. New York: Oxford University Press, 1966.

Wright, Arthur D. *Negro School Fund, Inc*. Washington, D. C.: The Negro Rural School Fund, Inc. 1933.

Zinn, Howard. *SNCC. Student Nonviolent Coordinating Committee: The New Abolitionists*. Boston: The Beacon Press, 1965.

Court Cases Cited

Adams v. *Richardson*. 480 F. 2d 1159 (1973).

Davis v. *Board of School Commissioners*. 402 U.S. 33 (1971).

DeFunis v. *Odegaard*. 416 U.S. 312 (1974).

Floyd v. *Trice*. 490 F. 2d 1154 (1974).

Green v. *County School Board of New Kent County, Virginia*. 391 U.S. 430 (1968).

Griffin v. *County School Board of Prince Edward County, Virginia*. 377 U.S. 218 (1964).

Hunnicutt v. *Burge*. 356 F. Supp. 1227 (1973).

Keys v. *School District No. 1, Denver, Colorado*. 413 U.S. 186 (1973).

Milliken v. *Bradley*. 94 S. Ct. 3112 (1974).

North Carolina Board of Education v. *Swann*. 402 U.S. 43 (1971).

Swann v. *Charlotte-Mecklenburg Board of Education*. 402 U.S. 1 (1971).